W9-AMC-686

The Complete Guide to
Duathlon Training

The following were involved in this book:
Dipl. oec. troph. Kirsten Brüning (chapter 14)
Katja Keiler (chapter 12) and
Dipl. Sportlehrer Martin Zülch (chapter 2-4 and 11)

Kuno Hottenrott

THE COMPLETE GUIDE TO DUATHLON TRAINING

Intelligently, Effectively, Successfully

Meyer & Meyer Sport

Original title: Duathlontraining
– 2., unveränderte Auflage – Aachen : Meyer und Meyer Verlag, 1996
Translated by Paul D. Chilvers-Grierson

Die Deutsche Bibliothek – CIP-Einheitsaufnahme

Hottenrott, Kuno:
The Complete Guide to Duathlon Training / Kuno Hottenrott. [Transl.: Paul Chilvers- Grierson]
– Aachen : Meyer und Meyer, 1998
Dt. Ausg. u.d.T.: Hottenrott, Kuno: Duathlontraining
ISBN 3-89124-530-0

All rights reserved. Except for use in a review, no part of this publication may be
reproduced, stored in a retrieval system, or transmitted, in any form or by any means now
known or hereafter invented without the prior written permission of the publisher. This
book may not be lent, resold, hired out or otherwise disposed of by way of trade in any
form, binding or cover other than that which is published, without the prior written
consent of the publisher.

© 1998 by Meyer & Meyer Sport, Aachen
Olten (CH), Vienna, Oxford,
Quebec, Lansing/ Michigan, Adelaide, Auckland, Johannesburg
www.meyer-meyer-sports.com
e-mail: verlag@meyer-meyer-sports.com
Cover Photo: Polar Electro GmbH, Büttelborn - Klein Gerau (right)
and M. Müller, Marburg (left)
Photos: LMT, Wallisellen (CH); V. Straub, Kassel; K. Hottenrott, Marburg;
Polar Electro GmbH, Büttelborn - Klein Gerau;
Mayaska Werbung, Mönchengladbach; S. Freiling, Kassel
Graphs/Drawings: K. Hottenrott und M. Dreesgrönemeyer, Marburg
Cover design: Walter Neumann, N&N Design-Studio, Aachen
Cover and Type exposure: frw, Reiner Wahlen, Aachen
Typesetting: Quay
Editorial: Dr. Irmgard Jaeger, Aachen, John Coghlan
Printing: Burg Verlag Gastinger GmbH, Stolberg
Printed in Germany
ISBN 3-89124-530-0

Contents

Foreword

In this book the author, an expert on the international duathlon/triathlon scene, provides in-depth training and race tips for all performance classes in duathlon. Athletes will find here a variety of proven training suggestions for all periods of the training year. In addition the endurance programmes are supplemented with selected functional stretching and strengthening exercises as well as comprehensive dietary recommendations appropriate to sport and for the use of the super compensation effect in preparing for an important race. In the chapter "Tests, Training and Performance Measurement" trainers, sports doctors and ambitious performance athletes are introduced to today's possibilities for regulating training through heart rate and lactate determination.

The book received much valuable input from co-authors whom I would hereby like to thank.

My special thanks go to the athletes Sonja Krolik (three times junior world champion in triathlon), Monika Böhl (several times GDR champion in cycling), Antje Saalfeld, Ralf Eggert (third placed in triathlon world championship, several times German champion in triathlon and duathlon), Normann Stadler (world champion in duathlon) and Carsten Wember (placed 6th and 8th in the German triathlon championships), who were actively involved in the illustrations and provided their experience from the fields of duathlon/triathlon/cycling. I also thank the company Polar Electro GmbH (Büttelborn – Klein Gerau near Frankfurt) for providing extensive photographic material and supporting the production of this book.

Dr. Kuno Hottenrott

1 The Fascination of Duathlon

More and more people are succumbing to the attractions of the still young sport of duathlon, which only in the eighties came out of the shadow of triathlon. Although in comparison to triathlon the sport does not have such an image-promoting location as Hawaii, the American Ken Souza provided duathlon with an absolute cult figure. The number of fans of the sport grew constantly in America, and as in so many other new sporting developments it was not long before the sport became popular beyond the borders of the American continent. The numerous attractive events in Germany (see ENGELHARDT 1994) motivated many athletes to participate in this double endurance sport. Its popularity here will certainly increase over the next few years, for world champion Normann Stadler has become a great idol locally.

As the Triathlon Sports Regulations (1994) do not permit swimming when the water temperature is below 15° C, it made sense, especially in countries with cool weather conditions, to carry out a combination of the endurance sports that left out swimming. The coupling together of running-cycling-running is attractive to a great number of athletes because of its requirements and the variety it offers, in particular for those who have had difficulty with the technically demanding discipline of swimming.

Duathlon can be practised both as a leisure and as a performance, or high performance, sport. It places correspondingly high demands on physical performance capacity or fitness, and in any case calls for consistent training. Figure 1 shows the most important factors which determine physical performance capacity.

In the system of activity known as sport there are factors over which the athletes themselves have no influence, such as e.g. their gender or genetically determined size, but also unchangeable environmental factors. Thus on race day it can rain or be very hot, the course can be unusually hilly or windy.

Athletes can influence their performance capacity in particular through training, diet and psychological attitude. It is the task of trainers and advisers in sports medicine to support them here. A performance, or high performance, athlete will not manage without this coaching and is dependent on the coach to a high degree. It is up to them to organise training with regard to type, intensity and amount, as well as measurement of the athlete's dietary and health condition. They are, however, also responsible, if for example the athlete lacks motivation or is nervous.

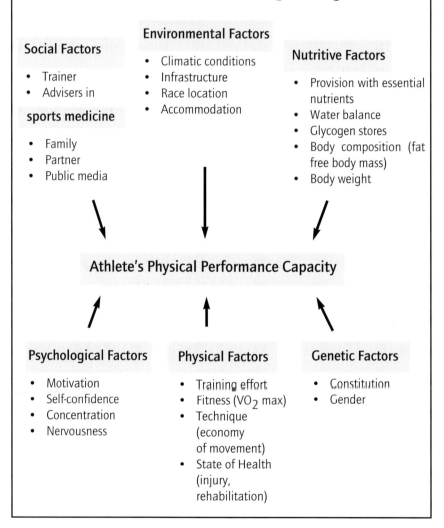

Factors Influencing the Athlete's Performance Capacity

Social Factors

- Trainer
- Advisers in

sports medicine

- Family
- Partner
- Public media

Environmental Factors

- Climatic conditions
- Infrastructure
- Race location
- Accommodation

Nutritive Factors

- Provision with essential nutrients
- Water balance
- Glycogen stores
- Body composition (fat free body mass)
- Body weight

Athlete's Physical Performance Capacity

Psychological Factors

- Motivation
- Self-confidence
- Concentration
- Nervousness

Physical Factors

- Training effort
- Fitness (VO_2 max)
- Technique (economy of movement)
- State of Health (injury, rehabilitation)

Genetic Factors

- Constitution
- Gender

Fig. 1: Factors influencing physical performance capacity

The social environment too plays a not unimportant role with regard to the athlete's performance capacity. A top athlete needs the support of his or her family and/or partner in order to be able to cope with the high demands of training and race performance.

Physical performance capacity is therefore dependent on a number of factors. If we transfer these general influences to the more specific race performance in duathlon, we get the following picture (Fig. 2):

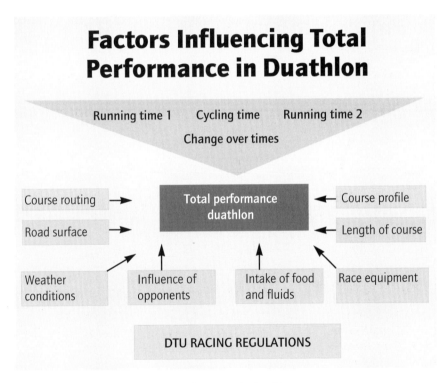

Factors Influencing Total Performance in Duathlon

Running time 1   Cycling time   Running time 2

Change over times

Course routing → | Total performance duathlon | ← Course profile

Road surface → | | ← Length of course

Weather conditions   Influence of opponents   Intake of food and fluids   Race equipment

DTU RACING REGULATIONS

Fig. 2: Factors influencing race performance in duathlon
(DTU = German Triathlon Union)

This book cannot deal intensively with all influencing factors. The emphasis here is placed on the physical factors. Training matters are covered, and the required knowledge is presented in a way which is easy to understand. Particular attention is devoted to effective training of fitness abilities, and further matters of training planning such as the cyclical planning of weekly training. Consideration is also given to the use of a performance increasing diet tuned specifically to training and race requirements.

In order to develop fitness abilities certain degrees of training effort must be realised. The amount of training effort cannot be chosen randomly, it is dependent among other things on current performance capacity, the number of years already trained, the amount of time available for training and the objectives. Only with these factors in mind can training be planned.

Training Hours per Year

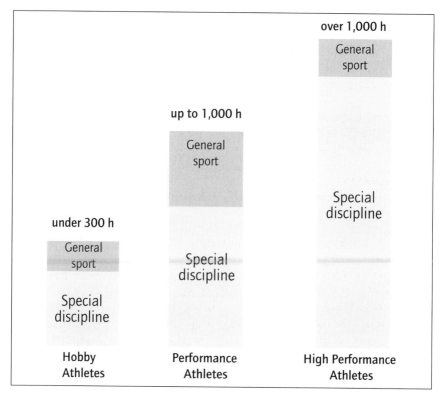

Fig. 3: Amount of training of Hobby (HA), Performance (PA) and High Performance (HPA) Athletes

The majority of duathletes train in pursuit of performance sport objectives and, in addition to their career and education, invest a great deal of time in training. The amount of training should not, however, be made so high that other important aspects of life are neglected. Generally, in relationship to performance objectives and the amount of training, three training groups can be differentiated from each other (Fig. 3):

- High Performance Athletes: They pursue duathlon professionally as their special discipline and train more than 1,000 hours per year (> 20 h/week). By doing so they create the prerequisites for top performances at international level.

- Performance Athletes: In their free time they train between 300 and 1,000 hours per year and aspire to regional and national success.

- Hobby Athletes: They usually practise several sports for health and fitness and as a psychological balance e.g to the demands of their job. Their sporting involvement is less than 300 hours per year. If they participate in races, then usually in novice and short duathlon races.

There are no statistics about the exact amount of training of the training group. The high level of performance demonstrated by duathletes in the various race classes suggests a great deal of hard work in training.

We know somewhat more about the amount of training of long-distance runners and cyclists. Professional cyclists cover over 40,000 km per year (an average of about 800 km per week).

In no other endurance sport do athletes train as much. This enormous number of kilometres represents the upper limit of an athlete's ability to endure effort. Top class long-distance runners train up to 8,000 km per year, the weekly distance is about 150 to 200 km. If the annual amount of training is converted into hours, it is much higher for cyclists than for long-distance runners. Running, on the other hand, places much higher demands on the supporting and moving system (SMS) than does cycling. Therefore further increases in the amount of effort in running are hardly possible.

Injuries to tendons, ligaments and joints would be the result. In the combination sport of duathlon these training loads are spread between two types of sport. This combats one-sided strain. As a rule there are less injuries among duathletes than amongst specialised athletes.

Annual Training Amounts in Duathlon

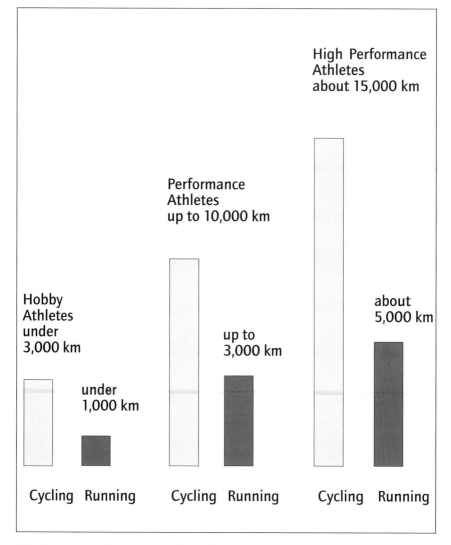

Fig. 4: Annual training amounts in duathlon

2 Effective Running Technique

An effective running technique is the basic prerequisite for high performance capacity. In duathlon there are roughly two running styles. The less advantageous – often observed as a result of adaptation difficulties after changing from cycling – features low speed, a "sitting" running position and little forward moving effect. The athlete practically falls passively into the forward supporting phase.

The technique duathletes should aim for is the so-called "rolling gait". In the forward supporting phase the foot is placed on the ground actively and with a pulling effect, with an active backwards movement of the leg in momentum. The foot touches the ground first at the heel bone. It then rolls through a light supination position over the outer instep to the ball of the small toe and then tips through a light pronation position to the ball of the big toe, which then provides the push off into the rear supporting phase. With increasing running speed the point where the foot first touches the ground moves forward – in a sprint only the front of the ball of the foot touches the ground (Fig. 5).
   In addition the upper body should support the running rhythm in a loose, relaxed posture. It is ideal if the upper body leans slightly forward.
The arms are swung loosely and bent alongside the body.

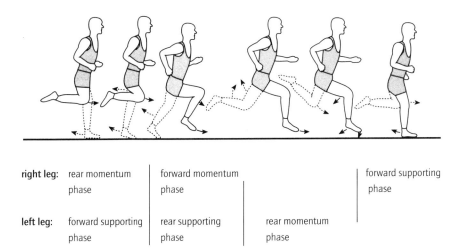

| **right leg:** | rear momentum phase | forward momentum phase | | forward supporting phase |
| **left leg:** | forward supporting phase | rear supporting phase | rear momentum phase | |

Fig. 5: Running technique (HOTTENROTT, ZÜLCH 1995)

An effective running technique is the basic prerequisite for high performance capacity.

Fascinating duathlon

Mountain biking – more and more popular with duathletes

Important: regular fluid intake

Standing on the pedals on a climb

Run & Bike

Running Technique Exercises (Running order)

The purpose of the running order is to improve and stabilise one's running style. Regularly carried out running exercises increase flexibility and strengthen the running muscles. Reduced proneness to injury is a positive side effect. There are less problems with muscles, tendons and ligaments.

An improvement in running style manifests itself in good coordination at higher running speeds, a higher variability of frequency and length of pace corresponding to the speed required, a relaxed running style even in a state of tiredness, and a delay in the development of tiredness.

Table 1 shows the running order exercises to be integrated in the warm-up in the order indicated. The movements should be carried out exactly as described.

Each exercise lasts about 20 seconds, about 15 to 30 metres are covered in each exercise. The break between exercises should be about 30 seconds.

Illustrations of the Running Order Exercises

◄ *Exercise 1:*
Ankle work with little raising of the knee

➤ *Exercise 2:*
Ankle work raising the knee higher

◄ *Exercise 3: Running with medium raising of the knee (skipping)*

➤ *Exercise 4a: Skipping with the knee raised high*

◄ *Exercise 4b: Skipping and kicking with the lower leg*

➤ *Exercise 5a: Roll off the heel*

◄ *Exercise 5b: Roll off the heel*

➤ *Exercise 6: Hopping run (vertical)*

◄ Exercise 7a:
Alternating jumps

➤ *Exercise 7b:*
Alternating jumps

◄ *Exercise 8:*
Running jumps

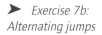

➤ *Exercise 9: Stretching*
jumps

◄ *Exercise 10a: Squat*
jumps with both legs

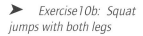

➤ *Exercise 10b: Squat*
jumps with both legs

◄ *Exercise 11: Cross legged running*

➤ *Exercise 12: Cross legged running with knee raised high*

Table 1: *Exercises, movement characteristics and mistakes in co-ordination and technique training in running (Sprint order)*

Exercise	Movement characteristics	Mistakes
1. Ankle work (normal/highest/increasing frequency)	○ Little raising of the knee with active placing of the foot on the ground in the direction of the body's centre of gravity (BCG)	○ Knee raised insufficiently/too high ○ Lack of stretching in the leg joints ○ Hanging toes
2. Ankle work with high knee raising on alternate sides	○ First stretching, then active placing of the foot on the ground on the forward supporting apparatus ○ Active support through co-ordinated arm movement	○ Not enough stretching in the leg joints ○ Passive placing of the foot on the ground on the forward supporting apparatus
3. Skipping a) normal/highest/increasing frequency b) Transition to running	○ Medium raising of the knee ○ Actively placing the ball of the foot in the direction of the BCG ○ Stretching in the leg and hip joints	○ Lack of stretching ○ Change in torso position in transition to running
4. Alternating between ankle work and skipping	○ Direct change over	○ Insufficient co-ordination of the individual movements in the various phases
5. Skipping (varying frequencies) a) knee raised high b) knee raised high with lower leg swinging out	○ Stretching ○ Body leaning forward ○ Arm movement in running direction in the direction of the BCG ○ Actively placing feet on ground ○ Co-ordination between arms and legs without twisting the torso	○ Knee raised insufficiently ○ Lack of stretching in the knee/hip joints ○ Passive swinging out and placing of the foot
6. Rolling off the heel a) onesided/alternating sides b) alternating sides with transition to running	○ Fast but relaxed swing through ○ Take upper leg back slightly ○ Arms in running direction	○ Hanging toes ○ Passive placing of the foot on the ground on the forward supporting apparatus ○ Tensed tearing away of the heels
7. Hopping run a) vertical direction of movement b) horizontal direction of movement with transition to running	○ Stretching in the leg and hip joints ○ Co-ordinated support by the arms ○ Active placing of the foot on the ground on the forward supporting apparatus in the direction of the BCG	○ Lack of stretching ○ Insufficient use of momentum elements ○ Rolling off the heel of the leg in momentum
8. Alternating jumps a) vertical/horizontal b) with transition to running	○ Stretching of the hip joints ○ Active placing of the foot ○ Arms in direction of movement	○ Lack of stretching ○ Passivity of leg in momentum ○ Uncoordinated transition to running
9. Running jumps a) with frequency b) with transition to running	○ Stretching and leading from the knee ○ Active placing of the leg in momentum in the direction of the BCG	○ Lack of stretching in the hip and knee joints ○ Passive landing on the forward supporting apparatus ○ Uncoordinated arm movement
10. Intensification of running (60-120 metres, high speed over 20-40 metres, then gradual "wind-down"), also as co-ordination intensification, i.e. the pace is constantly increased until running movement can only just be controlled well and corrected. In doing so attention is focused on a particular characteristic of running movement (e.g. stretching of the hips, raising of the knee or actively landing on the ball of the foot).		

Dolorita Fuchs-Gerber

Daniel Keller

3 Effective Cycling Technique

The most important foundation for effective foreward movement on a bike is a "rounded" pedalling technique. The higher the speed, the greater its significance. The more economically, and thus energy saving, one pedals i.e. revolutions per minute (r.p.m.), the faster and longer one can cycle at one's individual performance limit. A good pedalling technique saves energy.

One often sees beginners who pedal from above to below (chopping style). This constantly changes the angle at which energy is directed to the pedal; at the upper and lower points it is in fact zero. Although the pressure phase is decisive for driving forward, the other phases must also be carried out effectively, otherwise the pedalling becomes irregular and the pressure phase cannot be carried out at its best. The development of energy is at its greatest when the direction of the energy is channelled vertically onto the pedal. Altogether the pedalling cycle can be divided into four phases:

The basis for high performance in cycling is an aerodynamic position.

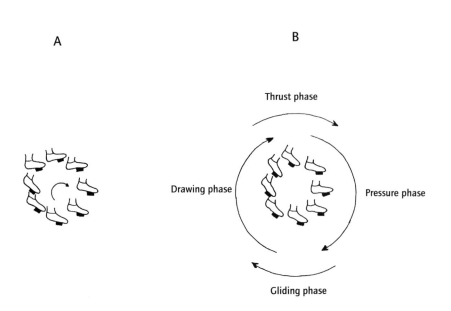

A   **B**

Fig. 6: Pedalling Cycle.
Illustration A shows uneconomical ankle work, while illustration B demonstrates an optimum angle of the upper ankle joint in all phases (modification of BURKE 1989, 95 and LINDNER 1993, 220).

Pressure phase – The phase in which the most energy is transferred. The pedalling movement is vertically downwards.

Gliding phase – The transition from the pressure to the drawing phase. The gliding phase is characterised by a pushing of the foot backwards and upwards with simultaneous stretching of the foot.

Drawing phase – The relaxing phase for the leg extensor muscles. During a medium stretching of the foot the leg draws backwards and upwards and thus supports the pressure phase.

Thrust phase – The transition from the drawing to the pressure phase. The thrust phase is characterised by a pushing forwards of the foot.

The constant change in the working muscles involved provides for the important relaxation phase, that is necessary to maintain performance at a high level.

It is the athlete's job to carry out the transitions between the individual phases as quickly and fluently as possible in order to achieve the optimum effect from the energy input. During pedalling the legs must work exactly parallel with each other like two connecting rods, otherwise too much pressure is placed on the knees which can lead to injuries. A clean style also manifests itself in such a way that the upper body and the head remain still while pedalling. In situations of extreme effort, however, such as sprints or steep hills, movement of the upper body cannot be avoided.

The right choice of gear and the right pedalling rate that goes with it have a decisive influence on performance. Speed will be higher the more one succeeds in cycling in the highest possible gear at the highest possible pedalling rate. The transition from cycling on a flat course, or even downhill, to climbing up hills often causes problems here. Athletes should change gear in such a way that there are no abrupt variations in pedalling rate.

Race judge checking a racing bike

Duathletes can develop a good cycling technique and high strength endurance on a mountain bike.

4 Functional Stretching and Strengthening Exercises

– in cooperation with Martin Zülch –

The stretching and strengthening exercises shown in this chapter are a basic programme for duathletes in all performance classes. They are directed at the mainly used muscle groups of the lower extremities and torso. On the following pages the names of the muscles, their locations in the body and the movement functions they have, are described.

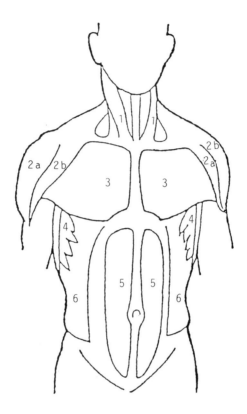

Body and shoulder muscles, seen from the front

1   Head turner (M. sternocleidomastoid): turns the head sideways.
2a Front shoulder muscle (M. deltoid anterior): raises the arm forwards.
2b Side shoulder muscle (M. deltoid lateralis): raises the arm horizontally sideways.
3   Large chest muscle (M. pectoralis major): lowers the arm from above towards the front.
4   Saw muscle (M. serratus): draws the shoulder blades forward and allows raising of the arm above the horizontal.
5   Straight stomach muscle (M. rectus abdominis) brings the thorax towards the pelvis, bending forwards.
6   Oblique inner and outer stomach muscle (M. obliquus abdominis externus et internus): allows sideways movement and turning of the torso.

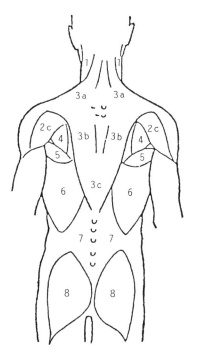

Back and shoulder muscles, seen from behind

1   Deep neck muscles: tip the head sideways and backwards.
2c Rear shoulder muscle (M. deltoid posterior): moves the arms horizontally backwards.
3a Hood muscle (M. trapezius), upper part: raises and holds the shoulders firm.
3b Hood muscle, middle part: brings the shoulders close to the spinal column.
3c Hood muscle, lower part: lowers the shoulder blades.
4   Small scapula muscle (M. teres minor): turns the arm outwards.
5   Large scapula muscle (M. teres major): with a slight inward turning movement it brings the arm close to the torso.
6   Broadest back muscle (M. latissimus dorsi): with a slight inwards rotation it draws the arm downwards from being held high.
7   Back extensor (M. erector spinae): keeps the spinal column straight.
8   Gluteal muscle (M. glutaeus maximus): stretches the leg from the hip.

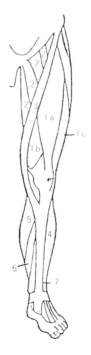

Leg muscles, seen from the front

1   Four-headed knee joint extensor (M. quadrizeps femoris): stretches the leg at the knee joint.
1a Straight thigh muscle (M. rectus femoris): stretches the knee joint.
1b Inner thigh muscle (M. vastus medialis): stretches and stabilises the knee joint.
1c Outer thigh muscle (M. vastus lateralis): stretches and stabilises the knee joint.
2   Thigh adductors: draw the leg to the centre of the body.
3   Tailor muscle (M. sartorius): turns the upper thigh outwards and the lower thigh inwards.
4   Front shin muscle (M. tibialis anterior): raises the foot at the ankle (dorsal flexor).
5   Twin calf muscles (M. gastrocnemius): stretches the foot at the ankle (plantar flexor).
6   Sole muscle (M. soleus): stretches the foot at the ankle (plantar flexor).
7   Toe extensor (M. extensor digitorum longus): helps with dorsal flexion.

```
       BOOKS-A-MILLION
     LAWNDALE SHOPPING CNTR.
     918 SOUTH GREEN RIVER RD.
      EVANSVILLE    IN   47715
STORE #0361    REGISTER #  1
1 02 RUNNERS WORLD            3.99
2 02 MUSCLE AND FITNESS'H     3.99
3 02 VELONEWS                 4.99
   SUB TOTAL    :    12.97
   CLUB DIS 10 %:     1.30-
SUB TOTAL       :    11.67
SALES TAX 5.000%:      .58
TOTAL           :    12.25
AMOUNT TENDERED :    12.25
CHANGE DUE      :
  2  CHECK             84
 14:53:41      7/21/02  CE
  YOU COULD BUY IT SOMEPLACE ELSE,
        BUT WHY PAY MORE?
     SAVE AN EXTRA 10% OFF
      EVERYTHING, EVERYDAY
     WITH YOUR DISCOUNT CARD!
--------- THANKS A MILLION ! ---------
YOUR CLUB MEMBERSHIP SAVED YOU    $1.36
```

Leg muscles, seen from behind

1   Large gluteal muscle (M. glutaeus maximus): stretches the leg in the hip.
2   Double-headed thigh flexor (M. biceps femoris): bends the leg at the knee and turns it outwards.
3   Half tendon muscle (M. semitendinosus): bends the leg at the knee and turns it inwards.
4   Flat tendon muscle (M. semimembranosus): bends the leg at the knee and turns it inwards.
5   Twin calf muscle (M. gastrocnemius): stretches the foot at the ankle (plantar flexor).
6   Sole muscle (M. soleus): supports the twin calf muscle.

Stretching and Strengthening Exercises

The individual muscle stretching and strengthening exercises are carried out before training sessions to prepare the body for high performance readiness. Increased joint mobility, coupled with better torso stability, ensures more economic movements over a longer period of endurance. Weak torso muscles, which do little to stabilise the vertebrae and the pelvis, work against economy of movement and forward driving energy, especially in a state of tiredness. Speed of movement is not only dependent on the muscles, joint mobility and the bone levers, but also on the stability of the torso (SOMMER et al. 1987, 1763).

After training sessions the stretching and strengthening exercises are carried out more intensively. They support the regeneration process, return muscles that tend to shorten to their original position, and strengthen the torso muscles which are barely used in endurance training. Regular stretching and strengthening is also the most effective protection against injury.

When doing the stretching and strengthening exercises make sure your movements are slow and not jerky (no bouncing or swinging). Stretch until you feel a slight twinge in the muscle. Maintain this position for 15-30 seconds. Repeat each stretching exercise two or three times, alternating exercises for the bending and stretching muscles.

Because the torso muscles mainly do holding work during endurance training, the strengthening exercises are carried out as isometric holding exercises. The maximum duration of an exercise is 60 seconds, but only as long as the athlete is capable of maintaining the correct end position. After a short relaxation phase the same exercise is repeated three to five times.

With a stretching and torso strengthening exercises ensure slow and controlled movements and even breathing.

Stretching the calf muscles (M. triceps surae)

Exercise 1: Stand before a wall with one leg forward and one back, both hands against the wall. To stretch the lower part of the thigh muscles (M. soleus) bend the back leg at the knee without raising the heel from the ground. To stretch the upper part of the calf muscle (M. gastocnemius) stretch the back leg at the knee – with the heel on the ground – and push the hips forwards.

◄ 1a

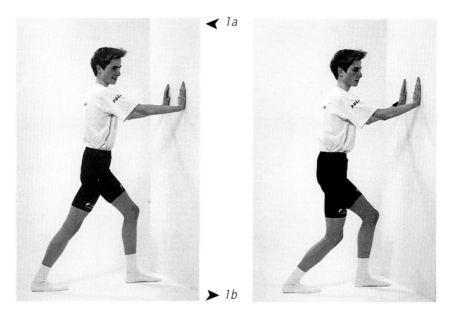

➤ 1b

Stretching the front shin muscles (M. tibialis anterior)

➤ Exercise 2:
Sitting on your heels, support yourself on hands placed next to the knees and raise your knees from the ground.

Stretching the front thigh muscles (M. quadriceps femoris)

◀ Exercise 3:
Standing on one leg slowly pull up a foot towards your buttocks with your hand, at the same time straightening your pelvis by tensing your buttock muscles (no compensatory movement of the pelvis).

Stretching the back thigh muscles (ischiocrural muscles)

◀ Exercise 4:
Lying on your back bend your leg at the knee, pull it towards your chest and clasp the back of your thigh with your hands. Then stretch the leg with the opposing muscles (knee extensor). In doing so tense the stomach and buttock muscles and press the lumbar vertebrae against the ground.

Stretching the back hip stretching muscles (M. glutaeus maximus)

➤ Exercise 5:
Standing on one leg clasp the bent knee with your hands and pull it to your chest. Keep your pelvis and torso straight by tensing the stomach and back muscles.

Stretching the hip bending muscles (M. iliopsoas)

➤ Exercise 6:
From a thrusting step (as in fencing) first push the hip forwards and downwards, hold it at the lowest point and then slowly stretch the back leg at the knee. In doing so avoid compensating with a hip movement backwards and upwards.

Stretching the back extensors (M. erector spinae)

◀ Exercise 7a:
Begin standing up straight, slowly roll the spine one vertebra at a time, letting your head and arms hang loosely. To increase the stretching bring your head in the direction of the hips by pulling it slightly. Then slowly unroll.

◀ Exercise 7b:
Active static stretching: Begin standing up straight, bend the torso forwards at a right angle. Actively stretch the arms out ahead. Hold your head as an extension of your spine. Arms, head and back form a straight line.

◀ Exercise 7c:
Passive static stretching: Begin as in exercise 7b. With outstretched arms the hands are placed e.g. on the shoulder blades of a partner. Stretch your back so far that the arms and back form a line.

➤ Exercise 7d:
Mobilisation: Starting from the bench position, alternate between arching and sagging your back.

Strengthening the torso muscles

➤ Exercise 8:
Stomach muscles: Lying on your back place your lumbar vertebrae firmly on the ground and raise your legs at a right angle. Then raise your chest, head and shoulders from the ground. Push your outstretched arms alongside your thighs. To strengthen the oblique stomach muscles draw your right arm and right shoulder to your left knee and vice versa.

◄ Exercise 9:
Lie on your back with your legs drawn up to a right angle. Then tense your buttocks and raise yourself so far from the ground that the body becomes a straight line.
Variation: During the tensing of the whole body alternately stretch the right and left lower legs at the knee.

◄ Exercise 10:
Lying on your stomach, raise your stretched legs, your head in extension of the spine, your shoulders and your arms stretched ahead a few centimetres from the ground. Maintain the tension for several seconds.

◄ Exercise 11:
Lying on your stomach and supporting yourself on your feet and your lower arms, raise your pelvis from the ground until the body is stretched out. Then alternately raise the left and right leg a maximum of one foot length above the ground. Do not compensate   with the pelvis (no hollow back).

Variation: (very demanding) Diagonally raise the right arm and the left leg, and vice versa, from the ground and hold them there for several seconds.

➤ Exercise 12:
Lying on your side and supporting yourself on your lower arm raise your hips so far from the ground that by tensing the torso, buttocks and leg muscles, the body forms a straight line. In doing so support yourself on the extreme edge of the lower foot.
Variation: Raise away the stretched upper leg and maintain the tension for several seconds.

➤ Exercise 13:
Stretching sitting position: Stretch your arms upwards and your feet forwards and straighten your spine.

5 Increasing Performance – How?

5.1 Training Concept

Improving sporting performance capacity requires optimum organisation of training. A training concept must be developed that deliberately orientates the training effort to the adaptations in the body. The cornerstones of the training concept are the expected performance in the training year (forecast performance), the specific demands of the sport (performance structure), and the current performance capacity of the athlete. The further training load is based on the five training components – amount, intensity, duration, density and carrying out of movement.

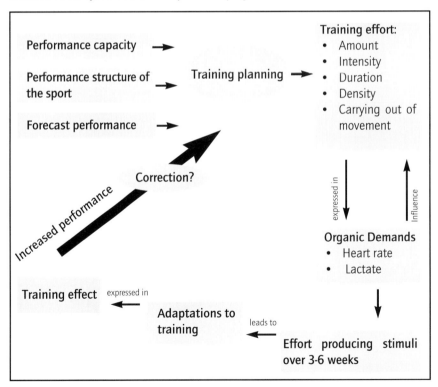

Fig. 7: Training concept – the basis of increasing performance

The *amount of effort* characterises the quantity of the planned or realised training in the various training sections and is usually expressed in hours or kilometres.

The *intensity of effort* characterises how strong the load is during training or racing. The demands on the body caused by the intensity of effort are determined by measuring the heart rate and lactate, among other things.

The *duration of effort* is the limiting of the training session or exercise series by time or by the distance covered.

The *density of effort* refers to the relationship between effort and recovery.

Effort is also differentiated according to the way *movements are carried out*. Thus the pedalling rate in cycling and the stride rate in running are used as methodical regulators of training effort.

The internal processing of efforts is referred to as demands placed on the body. In sport these demands are measured through the heart rate and the level of lactate. In high performance sport additional blood parameters such as urea and creatin kinase (cf. Fig. 59, p. 189f.) are measured. Every athlete processes or deals with training loads differently, i.e. they affect different athletes in different ways. The individual degree of endurance performance capacity has the greatest influence on the processing of effort. The higher the endurance performance capacity, the greater the load the athlete can handle.

Training leaves behind complex effects in the body which, according to duration, intensity and regularity of the movements carried out, places demands on a number of biological function systems and cause corresponding changes. Effort producing stimuli lead to short-term function system rearrangements in the body. This change in the level of regulation makes sense, for in this way the following training load can be handled with less effort. According to NEUMANN (1991, 50) physical loads producing stimuli applied over 3-6 weeks lead to organic adaptation which can manifest itself for example in increased size of the heart muscle, improved capillarisation, more mitochondria, increased storage of glycogen in the muscles and liver or more structural proteins in the skeletal muscles.

The adaptations caused by training thus express themselves in increased muscle strength, an increase in energy reserves or improved aerobic metabolism. This means that the athlete has increased his or her performance capacity and is now capable of dealing with increased training. Increased training in turn leads to increased demands on the organic systems, leading to further rearrangement and adaptation processes. Thus in a normal situation positive processing of stimuli will further increase performance capacity (figure 7).

5.2 Fitness Attributes Determining Performance

Endurance performance capacity is mainly determined by the fitness attributes: endurance, strength, speed and co-ordination. In terms of energy supply, endurance performance capacity can be divided into an aerobic and an anaerobic proportion.

Aerobic means that performance results from getting energy by burning oxygen, and anaerobic from getting energy without burning oxygen. This pure form of getting energy does not occur in endurance training; there is always a mixed metabolism with varying proportions of aerobic and anaerobic processes. In the uneconomical anaerobic way of getting energy, carbohydrates containing energy are fermented without oxygen, lactate arises as a waste product. It is therefore possible to use the measurement of the lactate concentration to determine how energy was gained during a particular form of training. Generally we consider a training session to be aerobic when the lactate concentration is under 2 mmol/l and as strongly anaerobic when it is over 6 mmol/l. Training to develop certain endurance capabilities is done in various training regions.

Endurance Capabilities
Determining Performance

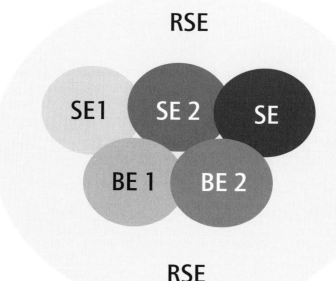

BE 1 and BE 2:	Basic Endurance Capability 1 and 2
SE 1 and SE 2:	Strength Endurance Ability 1 and 2
SE:	Speed Endurance Ability
RSE:	Race Specific Endurance Ability

Fig. 8: The fitness attributes determining performance in duathlon

Race specific endurance performance is mainly determined by basic endurance capability (BE 1 and BE 2), strength endurance capability (SE 1 and SE 2) and speed endurance capability (SE).

5.3 Principles of Effective Endurance Training

You can only achieve maximum effects if you train your body to best effect, i.e. if you neither undertax nor overtax it. Control of the use of stimuli that have a training effect is based on knowledge about the effects of demands on the body (cf. NEUMANN et al. 1991).

In this regard we can differentiate between four reactions:

1. Readjustment of the organic systems to the demands of a training session or a race

An athlete's organs and systems are capable of reacting to the specific demands of a sport. Endurance work leads to energetic deterioration processes (catabolic phase) and to tiredness which as a rule does not disappear until the next day. In this respect training can be seen as a planned disruption of an existing balance (homeostasis).

2. Restoration after effort of training or racing

In order to restore the functional state of the homeostasis the body tries to process the training stimulus. It does not only fully restore itself but, if the recovery phase is long enough, it refills the energy reserves beyond the starting level during this building up (anabolic) phase. This is referred to as super compensation.

3. Adaptation to training effort

If training stimuli are applied over a longer period of time, the body changes its normal level so that the pressure can be dealt with using as little effort as possible. Because the greater the remaining tiredness after training the more intensively the stimuli are processed, it is possible to influence the speed of the development in performance with appropriate systematic training.

Important here is the cyclical alternation between effort and recovery: in training, the stimuli are applied which instigate adaptation; in the recovery phase, the major adaptations then take place. The sum of many such training stimuli leads to constant adaptation and thus to performance improvement.

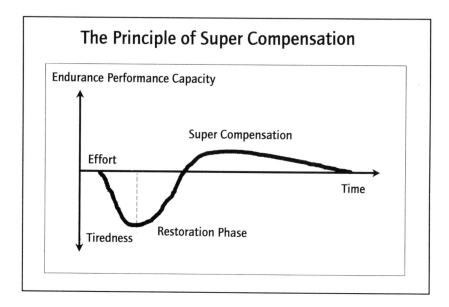

Fig. 9: The principle of super compensation (mod. acc. to JAKOLEW, 1977)

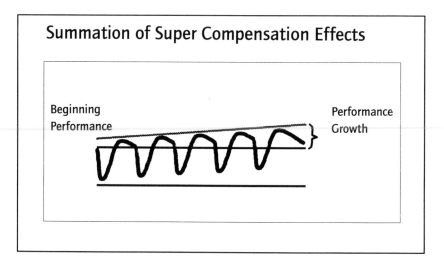

Fig. 10: Summation of super compensation effects in situation of progressive strain and optimum regeneration

4. Non-adaptation (overtaxing, overtraining)

A high level of training effort, strong psycho-physical stress, high glycogen consumption, high loss of minerals and vitamins, combined with a delayed refilling or microtraumatisation in muscle fibres and tissue, can hinder sufficient restoration of the body. In this case the desired adaptation and performance growth do not take place, rather there is a deterioration in sporting performance capacity.

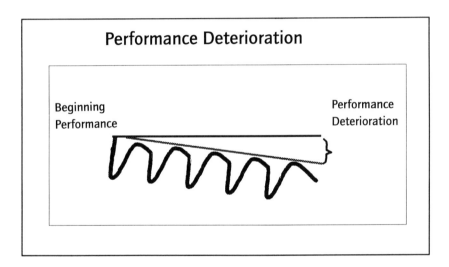

Fig. 11: Performance deterioration (explanation in text)

6 Individual Training Regions

Training regions define the intensity of effort under which the various training objectives are to be reached. In actual training three to four training regions are differentiated from one another for the development of endurance capabilities and two for the development of strength endurance capabilities.

The training regions must be individually worked out for every athlete. There are a number of possibilities for doing this which will be shown later. The safest orientation point for working out the training regions is the lactate concentration at a particular performance level.

Every sport has developed its own training regions. Table 2 gives an overview of the definition and terms of these in long-distance running, cycling and duathlon.

In the following the significance the individual training regions have for the development of sporting performance capacity is explained.

6.1 Regeneration and Compensation Training (RECOM Training)

In addition to measures for the development of endurance capability, measures are necessary for the restoration of sporting performance capacity after high training effort. Apart from physiotherapeutic measures (massages, hot baths) low-dosed sporting activity in various types of sport also helps. The aim of RECOM training is to accelerate the athlete's recovery and to create positive prerequisites for training loads that follow.

RECOM training in running = short, extensive jogging

Regenerative running includes short, extensive jogging up to a maximum of 45 minutes. The intensity of effort is very low and in the aerobic region, which means an upper heart rate of 60-70% of maximum heart rate.

By checking the upper heart rate limit you ensure that you do not enter too high a region of strain. A lower heart rate limit does not exist in regenerative running because the heart rate measurement is not intended to keep up the running pace but merely helps avoid too much strain.

Training Region	Metabolism	Intensity	Duathlon	Cycling*	Running
Regeneration Training	aerobic	very low	RECOM	CR	reg. Jogging
Basic Endurance Training	aerobic	low	BE 1	B 1	ext. Jogging
	aerobic/ anaerobic	medium	BE 1/2	B 2	int. Jogging
	aerobic/ anaerobic	high	BE 2	DR	SJ
Race Specific Endurance Training	strongly anaerobic	very high	RSE	TR	ext. SR/int.
Strength Endurance Training	aerobic anaerobic/ aerobic	medium high	SE 1 SE 2	S 3 S 2	– –

(*according to LINDNER 1993)

Table 2: Overview of the training regions and terminology of the endurance sports duathlon, cycling and running

Abbreviations: RECOM: Regeneration and compensation training; reg. Jogging: regenerative jogging; CR: compensation region; BE: Basic endurance training; B: Basic training; (ext. Jogging: extensive jogging, int. Jogging: intensive jogging), SJ: speed jogging; SR: speed run; DR: Development region; RSE: Racing specific endurance training; RE: Racing endurance training; TR: Top region; SE: Strength endurance training; S: Strength training.

Running on the beach strengthens the foot and leg muscles.

RECOM training in cycling = short, extensive cycling

Regenerative cycling includes short, extensive cycling up to a maximum of 90 minutes. The intensity of effort is very low and in the aerobic region, which means a heart rate of 60-70% of the maximum heart rate. For the upper and lower heart rate limit the same applies as to RECOM running.

6.2 Basic Endurance Training (BE Training)

For an improvement in race performance to take place there must first be an increase in basic endurance capability. It is the basis for higher race speeds in all endurance sports and is developed through BE training. Basic endurance training is aimed at an economising of the body systems and especially at maximum use of fat metabolism. To achieve this, two basic principles must be followed in basic endurance training:

1. BE training takes place all year round, with the emphasis in the preparatory periods.
2. The longer the training distance, the lower the intensity and vice versa.

Basic endurance training is further differentiated into BE 1, BE 1/2 and BE 2 training.

Basic Endurance Training 1 (BE 1)

It prepares high aerobic performance capacity of the systems for taking in, transporting and converting oxygen and is mainly carried out following the duration method. Altogether BE 1 training has a stabilising and economising effect on performance capacity.

The intensity of effort is regulated through the heart rate. The heart rate limits have a dual function here: the upper limit is used to avoid overtaxing, the lower limit as a driving force should the pace get too slow.

BE 1 Running = medium to long extensive jogging.
BE 1 running is carried out as medium (0:45-1:30 h) or long extensive jogging (over 1:30 h). The pace is higher than in RECOM running, and there should not be any over-acidity of the muscles.

BE 1 Cycling = medium to long extensive cycling.
BE 1 cycling is done as medium (1:30 to 3:00 h) and as long (over 3 h) extensive cycling. Pedalling rate is between 90 and 110 r.p.m. During the whole period under strain it must be ascertained that there is a high aerobic provision of energy with high mobilisation of fatty acids. On flat routes in particular the upper and lower heart rate limits force one to keep within the BE 1 region.

Basic Endurance Training 1/2 (BE 1/2)

BE 1/2 training is done at higher intensity and over a shorter duration. The intensity of effort is in the aerobic-anaerobic transitional region. The objective of BE 1/2 training is to develop basic endurance. It differs from BE 2 through a somewhat longer duration of effort at lower intensity.

BE 1/2 Running = short to medium intensive jogging.
BE 1/2 is carried out as short (0:30 to 0:45 h) and medium (0:45 to 1:30 h) intensive jogging.

BE 1/2 Cycling = short to medium intensive cycling.
BE 1/2 cycling is done as short (0:45 to 1:30 h) and as medium (1:30 to 3:00 h) intensive cycling. Pedalling rate is between 90 and 110 r.p.m.
DR Cycling = Cycling in the Development Region

BE 1 Running Training

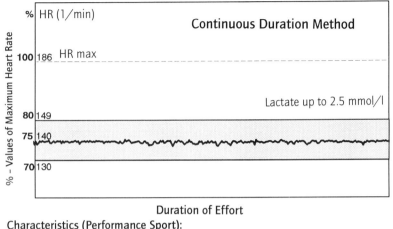

Characteristics (Performance Sport):
Duration of effort: over 45 min at even pace
Intensity of effort: 70-80 % of HR max, lactate 1.5 -2.0 mmol/l
Example: Runner with a maximum heart rate of 186 beats/min

Fig. 12: BE 1 Running following the continuous duration method with upper and lower heart rate limit

Basic Endurance Training 2 (BE 2)

BE 2 training requires partial use of the aerobic-anaerobic mixed metabolism. The body achieves a high lactate tolerance. Training is mainly by the alternating duration method and the intensive interval method. BE 2 training is also called "development training" (DR Training).

BE 2 Running = Fast Jogging.
The speed of fast jogging corresponds to the speed at the aerobic-anaerobic threshold. The upper and lower HR limits ensure that the intensity of effort is kept to. A BE 2 running session covers 3 to 12 km.

DR cycling = Cycling in the development region
Cycling in the development region leads to high demands on the body. The heart rate rises to 75-90 % of the maximum heart rate. At the same time lactate values of from 3-6 mmol/l are reached. If training is strength-oriented, pedalling rates are between 70 and 90 r.p.m., if frequency-oriented they are between 100 and 120 r.p.m.

BE 2 Running Training

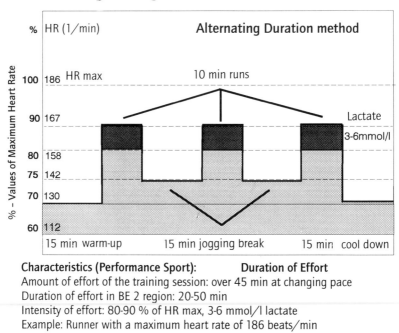

Characteristics (Performance Sport):   **Duration of Effort**
Amount of effort of the training session: over 45 min at changing pace
Duration of effort in BE 2 region: 20-50 min
Intensity of effort: 80-90 % of HR max, 3-6 mmol/l lactate
Example: Runner with a maximum heart rate of 186 beats/min

Fig. 13: BE 2 training according to the alternating duration method

6.3 Race Specific Endurance Training (RSE Training)

When the degree of the use of anaerobic-aerobic energy sourcing varies, race specific endurance capability ensures maximum race speed over courses of various lengths. The development of race specific endurance capability occurs through race specific endurance training (RSE).

Training is mainly carried out according to the interval, repetition and race method at speeds and distances that approximate those of races.

If training is at speeds higher than average race speeds, then lower than race distance loads should be chosen where quick carrying out of movements is important (e.g. high pedalling rate) and vice versa.

RSE Running = extensive and intensive fast running.
Extensive fast runs are runs at submaximum speed over 300 to 2,000 m. The total amount in a training session is between 2 and 6 km (e.g.: 10 x 200 m or 8 x 1,000 m). Intensive fast runs are interval runs over 50 to 300 m at almost maximum speed.

TR Cycling = Cycling in the top region.
In TR cycling submaximum to maximum speeds are reached over relatively short distance sectors. The individual sector for TR training is between 100 and 6,000 m. The shorter the distance, the higher the speed and the longer the breaks. TR cycling training is done at pedalling rate between 80 and 130 r.p.m.

In RSE/TR training the heart rate (HR) plays a lesser role as a determinant of intensity of effort. The intensity determinant is mainly reached as a result of speed measured in field tests or race tests. HR regulation is of particular importance in the recovery phases. The breaks are determined using the steepness of the HR drop. For example the period of effort only begins when the recovery HR has reached 120 beats/min.

That can take two to five minutes. Yet even when the length of the breaks is constant the recovery HR gives information about the degree of tiredness.

If between the periods of effort there is a delayed decrease in the recovery HR then either the recovery time is too short or the intensity is too high. Changes in the training programme should be carried out straight away.

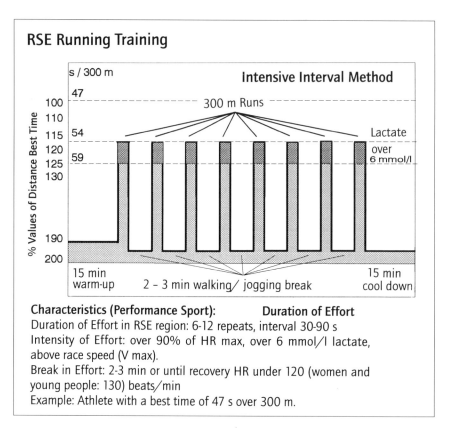

RSE Running Training

Intensive Interval Method

s / 300 m

% Values of Distance Best Time

300 m Runs

Lactate over 6 mmol/l

15 min warm-up   2 - 3 min walking/ jogging break   15 min cool down

Characteristics (Performance Sport):   Duration of Effort
Duration of Effort in RSE region: 6-12 repeats, interval 30-90 s
Intensity of Effort: over 90% of HR max, over 6 mmol/l lactate, above race speed (V max).
Break in Effort: 2-3 min or until recovery HR under 120 (women and young people: 130) beats/min
Example: Athlete with a best time of 47 s over 300 m.

Fig. 14: RSE training: 300 m fast runs according to the intensive interval method

6.4 Specific Strength Endurance Training (SE Training)

In addition to basic endurance training, strength training is another performance reserve. Maximum and semi-specific strength abilities are trained in the preparatory period doing circuit and station training with and without machines. Comprehensive recommendations on this can be found in Chapter 11.

Specific strength endurance training is divided into two regions of intensity called SE 1 and SE 2. The objective of strength endurance training is to increase the amount of drive forward per movement cycle and also the ability to resist tiredness.

Strength Endurance Training 1 (SE 1)

It develops and stabilises high aerobic strength endurance capability and is mainly trained using the (alternating) duration method and extensive interval method.

SE 1 Running = medium, extensive hill running.
The SE 1 run is carried out as a medium (up to 1:00 h) extensive hill run. The intensity of effort is between 75-85 % of maximum heart rate.

   The muscles should not become over-acidic, i.e. lactate should not rise above 3 mmol/l. The length of stride decreases in relation to the steepness and is considerably shorter than on flat land.

SE 1 Cycling = extensive, medium cycling.
SE 1 cycling is done as medium (up to 3:00 h) extensive cycling on flat land or on hills of medium steepness.

   The intensity of effort is the same as in SE 1 running. Pedalling rate is considerably less than in BE 1 training at 50-70 r.p.m.

Strength Endurance Training 2 (SE 2)

It develops maximum strength endurance ability and is carried out using the intensive interval method, the repetition method or the Fartlek method. The intensity of effort is high and rises to up to 95% of maximum heart rate. Demand on the muscles is strongly anaerobic at high lactate concentrations of 4-7 mmol/l.

SE 2 Running = intensive hill or stair run.
Example of intensive stair running: after warming-up, a stairway of more than 50 steps is run up several times at a high intensity of effort.

   During each run certain tasks can be allotted, such as jumping over 3-5 steps at once, one-legged jumps, (two-legged) final jumps. After each individual period of effort there is an active break of at least two minutes. The number of repetitions depends on the fitness of the athlete.

Intensive hill running is done several times at a high intensity of effort on steep slopes of at least 30 m in length. Active recovery is at least two minutes.

SE 2 Hill Cycling = short, intensive hill cycling.
Short, steep slopes are cycled up several times at 40-70 r.p.m. at high intensity (see SE 2 Running). The recovery phase between the sections is about 3-5 min.

Training Regions

	RECOM Training	BE 1 Training	BE 2 Training	RSE Training	SE 1 Training	SE 2 Training
Objective	• Support of restoration ability for the following intensive training load • Increase mobilisation	• Stabilisation and development of basic endurance capability • Increase aerobic capacity	• Development of basic endurance capability • Increase aerobic capacity	• Intensifying race specific endurance capability	• Development and stabilisation of aerobic strength endurance capability	• Development of maximum strength endurance capability
Method	• Duration method	• Duration method • Fartlek method	• Extensive interval method • Fartlek method • Alternating duration method	• Race method • Intensive interval method • Repetition method	• Duration method • Alternating duration method • Extensive interval method	• Intensive interval method • Repetition method • Fartlek method
Intensity	• very low • Lactate: below 2.0 mmol/l	• low-medium • Lactate: up to 2.0 mmol/l up to 3.0 (BE 1/2)	• medium-high • Lactate: 3.0-6.0 mmol/l	• high-very high • Lactate: over 6.0 mmol/l	• medium • Lactate: 2.0-3.0 mmol/l	• high • Lactate: 4.0-7.0 mmol/l
Running	60-70% of HR max	70-80% of HR max 75-85% (BE 1/2)	80-90% of HR max	> 90% of HR max	75-85% of HR max	85-95% of HR max
Cycling	60-70% of HR max	65-75% of HR max 70-80% (BE 1/2)	75-90% of HR max	> 90% of HR max	75-85% of HR max	85-95% of HR max
Pedalling rate	80-100 r.p.m.	90-110 r.p.m.	70-90 r.p.m. strength-oriented 100-120 r.p.m. frequency-oriented	80-130 r.p.m.	50-70 r.p.m.	40-60 r.p.m.

3: Summary of the objectives, methods and intensities for the individual training regions (RECOM: Regeneration and Compensation Training; BE: Basic Endurance Training; RSE: Race Specific Endurance Training; SE: Strength Endurance Training)

7   Tests, Training and Performance Measurement

7.1 Heart Rate

In order to train effectively it is necessary to find out the individually correct intensity of effort. Very few athletes using their subjective feeling for their body manage to do this. Often development of performance is not possible because the training intensity is usually too great, but sometimes also because it is too low. Measuring the heart rate can help clear up this uncertainty.

Before beginning to measure the heart rate in training, certain basic knowledge is necessary. This includes:

1:    Knowledge about the heart rate at rest, under strain and during recovery.
2.   Ways of determining the upper and lower heart rate limits in the training regions.
3.   Particular symptoms of the heart rate and their significance for training.

7.1.1 Resting Heart Rate, under Strain and during Recovery

For determining intensity, carrying out and measurement of training loads, four heart rate parameters are important:

1.   Resting heart rate
2.   Training heart rate
3.   Maximum heart rate
4.   Recovery heart rate

Resting Heart Rate

The resting heart rate should be measured early in the morning directly after waking up, lying down. An adult's resting HR is about 70 beats/min. Endurance training leads to a lowering of the resting HR. Performance athletes usually have a resting HR of 50 beats/min. High performance athletes have a rate 10 to 15 beats/min. lower.

Measuring the resting HR is especially important for monitoring one's state of health. First signs of health disruption, such as influenza infections, are expressed in a rise in the heart rate. If the morning resting HR is significantly up (more than 8-10 beats/min.) then you should only train at low intensity (RECOM region).

Training Heart Rate

The training HR has great practical significance in judging the degree of physical effort. Manual pulse measurement (at the wrist or neck) is not accurate enough for exact regulation of intensity of effort.

Comparisons of manual pulse measurement with exact ECG methods have shown that manual measurement differs from the real heart rate by 8 to 12 beats/min.

Training Heart Rate in Relationship to Age and Duration of Effort

Table 4 and table 5 show recommendations for optimum intensity of effort in running and cycling based on the heart rate. The intensity is determined in relationship to age and the duration of the training session. In this way overtaxing can thus be avoided for the most part. For cycling a longer duration of effort is recommended than for running because here the level of organic demand is lower over the same period. Because cyclists are more subject to external influences (wind, route profile), table 5 suggests a higher HR region for determining the intensity of effort.

By constantly measuring the heart rate (Polar Electro) it is possible to keep exactly to the set intensity of effort.

Table 4: *Upper and lower limits of the heart rate (HR) for developing basic endurance in running*

The training HR varies depending on age and duration of effort. It goes down with increasing age and duration. In BE 1 training, top athletes go below the lower limit values. HR values in beats/min (according to NEUMANN/PFÜTZNER/HOTTENROTT 1993).

| Age (Years) | Duration of Effort in long-distance Running | | |
	up to 45 min	up to 90 min	over 90 min
under 15	180 – 170	175 – 165	170 – 160
15 – 20	165 – 155	160 – 150	155 – 145
20 – 30	155 – 145	150 – 140	145 – 135
30 – 40	150 – 140	145 – 135	140 – 130
40 – 50	145 – 135	140 – 130	135 – 125
50 – 60	140 – 130	135 – 125	130 – 120
over 60	135 – 125	130 – 120	125 – 115

Table 5: *Upper and lower limits of the heart rate (HR) for developing basic endurance in cycling*

The training HR varies depending on age and duration of effort. It goes down with increasing age and duration. In BE 1 training top athletes go below the lower limit values. HR values in beats/min (according to NEUMANN/PFÜTZNER/HOTTENROTT 1993).

| Age (Years) | Duration of Effort in Cycling | | |
	up to 90 min	up to 150 min	over 150 min
under 15	150 – 170	145 – 165	140 – 160
15 – 20	145 – 160	140 – 155	135 – 150
20 – 30	140 – 155	135 – 150	130 – 145
30 – 40	135 – 150	130 – 145	125 – 140
40 – 50	130 – 145	125 – 140	120 – 135
50 – 60	125 – 140	120 – 135	115 – 130
over 60	120 – 135	115 130	110 – 125

Maximum Heart Rate

The maximum heart rate is of great significance as a starting point for training heart rates which are determined using it. It is dependent on age, sex, preparedness for performance and muscular mobilisation ability. Children effortlessly reach 200 beats/min. Women too tend to have higher heart rates so that female athletes have a heart rate about 10 beats/min higer than males at the same level of performance.

The heart rate value determined using the formula "maximum heart rate = 220 – age in years" can only be a rough guideline in determining the level of intensity because this value usually differs considerably from the actual maximum heart rate. Training intensities can be determined more exactly if the maximum HR is ascertained using an endurance test and checked at regular intervals (3 – 6 weeks). For the "maximum test" it is recommended to follow a sufficiently long warm-up phase of about 20

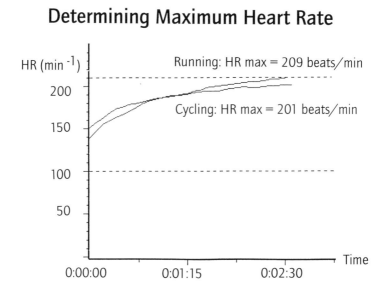

Determining Maximum Heart Rate

Running: HR max = 209 beats/min
Cycling: HR max = 201 beats/min

HR (min⁻¹)

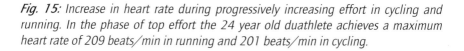

Fig. 15: Increase in heart rate during progressively increasing effort in cycling and running. In the phase of top effort the 24 year old duathlete achieves a maximum heart rate of 209 beats/min in running and 201 beats/min in cycling.

minutes with a progressive increase of effort up to maximum speed (e.g. 1,000 m running or 2,000 m cycling). The prerequisite for the test is a healthy state and that from a medical point of view there is no reason for not doing the test.

When ascertaining the maximum HR it can happen that because of a great deal of exclusively aerobic endurance training over several weeks, or after high training intensity the day before, it is not possible to get full activation of the heart and circulatory system and thus the maximum heart rate is not reached. This must be taken into consideration when determining intensity of effort using the maximum HR.

Recovery Heart Rate

The training state can be assessed using the heart rate decrease when effort is ended (=recovery HR). The higher the performance capacity, i.e. the fitter the athlete is, the faster the heart and circulatory system recovers from the activity just ended. The recovery heart rate is a fine measurement of regeneration capability. After heavy sporting load, or overexertion, there is a delay in the drop in the heart rate. In the first recovery minute after maximum effort performance athletes' heart rates fall by an average of 35 beats/min.

After three recovery minutes they reach values of under 110 beats/min. Further reduction of the heart rate until the starting or resting rate is reached can take hours. The more the effort has affected metabolic processes, the slower the return to the starting HR takes place.

7.1.2 Conconi Test

If it is desired to individually determine the training regions from the heart rate behaviour only, i.e. independent of lactate measurements, this is possible using the Conconi test.

The Conconi test is based on the phenomenon that in the region of about 120-170 beats/min, in some cases up to 190 beats/min, the HR behaves in a linear relationship to effort. When the performance demands rise further, the HR values move away from the linear relationship.

This break off, or deflection point, was named by CONCONI and colleagues (1982) as Pd (pulse deflection) and Vd (velocity deflection) and characterises the anaerobic threshold.

Test Instructions

The Conconi test has proved itself more in light athletic running than in cycling. In running the test is carried out on a 200 m or 400 m track. After every 200 m the runnig time and the heart rate are registered with the Sport Tester; further markings – e.g. every 50 m – can be used to regulate and check running speed (Fig. 16).

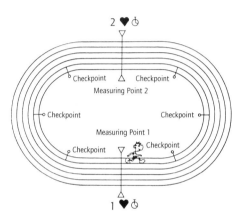

The test always begins with an approximately ten minute long warm-up phase (slow jogging). In this phase the heart rate should not rise above 130 beats/min. In relation to fitness the starting speed should be chosen in such a way that the athlete can go through at least eight effort sectors (1,600 m). Athletes with a 10 km best time between 32 min and 38 min can begin at a speed of 12 km/h (=60 s over 200 m). Those who have trained more can select a higher speed, less

Fig. 16: Test arrangements for the Conconi test

well-trained people choose a lower speed. Independent of the starting speed, every 200 m the pace is increased by 0.5 km/h. In this way at every level of effort work remains a product of performance and time. In the past the "Conconi test structure" has been used in a number of research projects not in its original form, but in some cases considerably modified, which led to irritations and contradictory results.

   There are several possibilities for exactly regulating running speed:

1.   An acoustic signal every 10 m according to the rhythm of Heart Rate Control Software (HRCT)
2.   Running tables with set times for every 50 m (see Table 6)
3.   Conconi test on a treadmill with fully automatic speed regulation, increasing by 0.5 km/h after every 200 m.

Carrying out the test is simple when a HR measuring device with memory (Sport Tester "Profi" from Polar Electro) is available. In this case it is recommended to take the heart rate at five second intervals. The test is completed when, in correlation to the set speed, as much effort as can be handled has been experienced.

Final preparations for the race

Cycling in duathlon

German women's champion in duathlon

Racing with heart rate measurement

Training with heart rate measurement

Table 6: *Running table for the Conconi test. The figures emphasised represent the sum of the target times at the 200 m measuring points; the smaller figures serve as a check over the 50 m partial sectors.*

		0 to 1,000 m	1,000 to 2,000 m	2,000 to 3,000 m	3,000 to 4,000 m
50 m →		0:15	4:49,6	8:40.6	11:59.4
		0:30	5:02,2	8:51.2	12:08.6
		0:45	5:14,5	9:01.7	12:17.8
200 m →		1:00,0	5:27,0	9:12.3	12:27,1
		1:14,4	5:38,9	9:22.6	12:36.1
		1:28,8	5:50,9	9:32.9	12:45.1
		1:43,1	6:02,9	9:43.1	12:54.1
400 m →		1:57,5	6:15,0	9:53,4	13:03,1
		2:11,3	6:28,5	10:03.4	13:11.9
		2:25,1	6:38,1	10:13.4	13:20.7
		2:38,8	6:49,7	10:23.4	13:29.5
600 m →		2:52,5	7:01,4	10:33,4	13:38,2
		3:05,8	7:12,7	10:43.1	13:46.8
		3:19,1	7:24,0	10:52.8	13:55.4
		3:32,4	7:35,2	11:02.6	14:03.9
800 m →		3:45,8	7:46,4	11:12,3	14:12,5
		3:58,6	7:57,3	11:21.8	14:20.9
		4:11,5	8:08,2	11:31.1	14:29.3
		4:24,3	8:19,1	11:40.8	14:37.6
1000 m →		4:37,2	8:30,0	11:50,2	14:46,0

Test Evaluation

Manual Evaluation

The data lists (table 7) give an overview of the recorded HR values and interim times. In manual evaluation it is not necessary to memorise all the values. The HR values at the end of each 200 m stage and the times between are sufficient. These values are entered on a record sheet (table 8).

This first step is followed by a conversion of the 200 m time to km/h using the formula: v (km/h) = (720/time in seconds over 200 m).

The third step is to plot the co-ordinates (HR, speed) on a graph with the heart rate on the y axis and speed on the x axis. When all the positions have been entered a compensatory line can be plotted in the linear region (Fig. 17). The points in the upper HR region are usually outside the linear heart rate line. The so-called point of deflection (other terms for this: break off point, turning point) characterises the anaerobic "Conconi threshold". This differs from the anaerobic „lactate Threshold".

Table 7: *Data list of the values saved in the Sport Tester "Profi" (total time, < >: time in s over 200 m and heart rate in beats/min., calculated from the heartbeats over 5 s in each case).*

```
0 min. 0.0 s  HR 118 (0 s)
122    127    127    127  138  140  141  141  142  143  145  146
1 min. 0.3 s (60.3 s)
149    152    153    154  153  152  152  153  154  155  155
1 min. 57.5 s (57.2 s)
155    157    158    158  159  160  161  161  161  161  161
2 min. 52.6 s (55.1 s)
162    162    163    163  164  163  163  165  167  167  166
3min. 45.6 s (53 s)
166    166    167    169  169  169  169  169  169  169
4 min. 37.3 s (51.7 s)
170    172    172    173  173  172  171  172  173  174
5 min. 27.3 s (50 s)
173    175    174    175  174  174  176  174  174  175
6 min. 15.4 s (48.1 s)
173    178    178    178  179  179  177  179  179
7 min. 1.7 s (46.3 s)
179    178    179    180  181  181  181  181  180
7 min. 46.7 s (45 s)
179    181    182    183  182  183  182  181  181
8 min. 30.3 s (43.6 s)
182    183    183    182  182  181  183  182
9 min. 12.6 s (42.3 s)
185    186    184    183  182  183  183  184
9 min. 53.3 s (40.1 s)
196    185    184    185  185  188  187  186
10 min. 33.4 s (40.1 s)
188    187    188    187  187  189  187  188
11 min. 11.3 s (37.9 s)
187    187    184    180  177  175  173  170  165  161  158  156  154  150  148  147
145    144    141    139  136  135  132  130  129  128  126  125  123  122  120  120
```

Manual evaluation of the Conconi test: the values are recorded and then displayed in a graph.

Table 8: Record sheet for evaluation of the Conconi test (distance: distance covered in metres since the start; time: 200 m time in s; HR: heart rate at end of the 200 m distance; V: speed in km/h over 200 m, calculated with the formula: V = (720/time in s over 200 m)

Record Sheet

Name: ....   Date: ....

Age: ....   Temperature: ....

Distance (m)	Time (s)	HR (min-1)	V (km/h)	Remarks
200	60,3	146	11,9	
400	57,2	155	12,6	
600	55,1	161	13,1	
800	53,0	166	13,6	
1,000	51,7	169	13,9	
1,200	50,0	174	14,4	
1,400	48,1	175	15,0	
1,600	46,3	179	15,6	
1,800	45,0	180	16,0	
2,000	43,6	181	16,5	
2,200	42,3	182	17,0	
2,400	40,7	184	17,7	
2,600	40,1	186	18,0	
2,800	37,9	188	19,0	

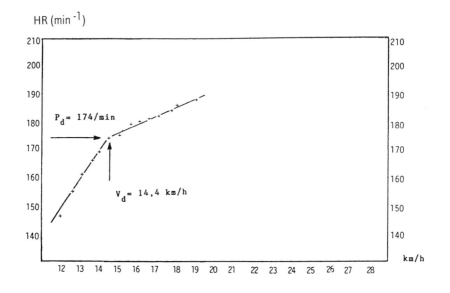

Fig. 17: Heart rate-speed curve with compensating line in the upper and lower HR region and "Conconi threshold"

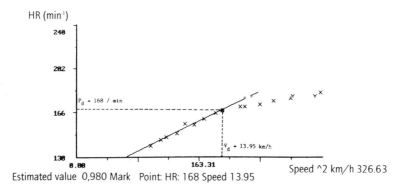

Estimated value 0,980 Mark Point: HR: 168 Speed 13.95

Fig. 18: Graphic evaluation of a Conconi test using software from Polar Electric. The graph shows the relationship heart rate-speed and the "Conconi threshold" at a HR of 168 beats/min and a speed of 13.41 km/h.

Evaluation with POLAR software

If it is possible to transfer the recorded data to a personal computer, the evaluation can be carried out very easily using POLAR software (Fig. 18). The programme simultaneously calculates the aerobic and anaerobic "Conconi threshold" and provides the upper HR value and the speed for various training intensity levels (Table 9).

Table 9: Tabular evaluation of the Conconi test with software from Polar Electric. The anaerobic and aerobic limit for the heart rate and speed as well as the maximum test performance (upper limit) were calculated.

CONCONI TEST		Copyright by Polar Electric	
	Upper limit	Anaerobic limit	Aerobic limit
Heart rate (min-1)	194	180	160
Speed (m/s)	5.28	4.28	3.59
Speed (km/h)	19.00	15.41	12.94
Time (min/km)	03:09	03:53	04:38
Time (min/mile)	05:04	06:16	07:27
Lap length.................................200 m			
Total time (min)....................14:23.8			
Number of interim times....................15			
Degree of speed......................................3			
Source...A:\CT061191.RAW			

Start of a Conconi test

Determining the Training Regions

The individual speed for running training is derived as a percentage of heart rate and speed at the deflection point in the Conconi test. The percentage values for HR and speed are not identical in the various training regions.

This is explained by the fact that as a rule the HR-speed curve does not coincide with the identity line (45° gradient).

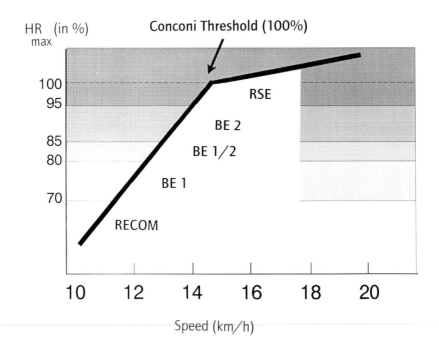

Fig. 19: *Heart rates for running training in the RECOM, BE 1, BE 1/2, BE 2 and RSE regions*

7.1.3 Particular Heart Rate Reactions

The following shows heart frequency phenomena which occur in training and possible causes and consequences for training.

Phenomenon/Observation	Possible Cause	Training Measure
• Rest HR is greatly increased	• Overtaxing • Overtraining • Infection	• Reduction of training • Break from training
• In speed training the HR does not reach the usual value	• Overtraining • Glycogen impoverishment	• No speed training • More BE 1 training
• The HR max is not reached in the test	• Glycogen impoverishment • Low muscle mobilisation	• Reduction of amount • Starts, slopes and sprints
• The HR remains unusually high in the breaks during interval training	• Pace is too high	• Reduce pace • Extend the breaks • Stop training
• The HR remains high hours after training	• Exhaustion • Lack of fluids	• Regenerative measures • Drink fluids
• The HR rises unusually fast at the same pace	• Loss of fluids • Infection	• Stop training • Drink fluids

*) According to SCHÜTZ (1958), when a person has a fever an increase in heart rate of 8-10 beats/min per 1° C can be asertained.

7.1.4 Factors Influencing Heart Rate

In sport the heart rate can be measured at any time with ECG exactness using wearable heart rate watches (e.g. "Sport Tester" from Polar Electro). In addition to sporting effort, it is affected by a number of other factors which can make an interpretation of the values measured difficult. Only those who know the influencing factors can correctly interpret the heart rate values measured.

Temperature and Humidity
The increase in body temperature has the greatest effect on the heart rate. This can increase by 2-3° C during training at high temperatures (> 30° C), in high humidity (> 70%) and with insufficient fluid intake. At the same performance level the heart rate would be 15-20 beats/min higher in comparison to normal conditions.

Quick changes in climate always have a greater effect on the heart rate than slow changes, for the body is capable of adapting to changing conditions. This fact must be especially taken into consideration when races take place in other climatic zones. The journey to the race location should therefore take place 5-10 days earlier.

Food Intake
Food intake increases the heart rate, e.g. after a main meal by 10-20 beats/min. On the other hand the heart rate sinks in a long lasting state of hunger.

Influence of the Daily Rhythm
The daily variations in the heart rate are closely related to food intake, sporting activity and one's physical and psychological state.

7.2 Lactate

7.2.1 Measurement of Lactate in Sport

Lactate, the salt of lactic acid in the blood, is the final product of anaerobic metabolism. It mainly arises during intensive muscle activity from the breakdown of glucose. A high percentage of the lactate formed during exercise goes into the blood. It is removed by various organs such as the liver, the heart muscle and the skeletal muscles.

In a state of rest the lactate concentration in the blood is 1-2 mmol/l. When more lactate arises it is always a sign that the muscles used are not using enough oxygen to release energy.

Lactate determination has attained great significance in endurance training. After the heart rate it is the most used monitoring instrument for the optimisation of training. In future its significance will increase and it will not just be primarily for high performance athletes, as has so far been the case. The foundations for this have already been laid: using a portable device for quick lactate measurement ("Accusport") every athlete can determine the lactate concentration in their own blood. Here too the fast availability of medical data is the prerequisite for effectively measured training.

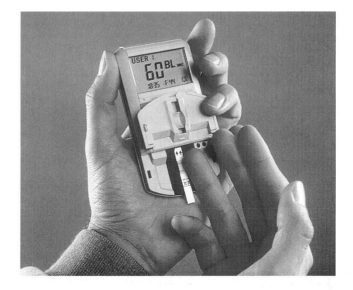

"Accusport", a portable device for quick lactate measurement made by Hestia.

7.2.2 Staggered Field Tests with Lactate Determination

Successful endurance training depends to a great degree on the "right" amount of effort. The training loads must not be too high or too low. Underuse of the body does not lead to adaptation, overuse results in decreased performance. In order to find the individually optimal amount it is necessary to determine exactly the aerobic and anaerobic threshold. The following field tests have proven useful for performance training in long-distance running and cycling:

long-distance running: 4 – 6 x 2,000 – 3,000 m
Road cycling: 4 – 6 x 4,000 – 6,000 m

Carrying Out The Test
In each stage of training the pace remains constant. The pace in the first stage must be determined in relationship to the fitness of the athlete. It must be ascertained that it remains in the aerobic region. The final stage of training can take the athlete to the limits. After each stage a lactate measurement is carried out as well as measurement of the heart rate under strain. The data gathered is then put into a lactate-heart rate or lactate-speed diagram. From this the training regions can be worked out (Fig. 20).

Cycling Field Test
The intensity of effort at each stage can be regulated both by speed and by heart rate. In practice the HR is set for each stage in relation to the individual maximum heart rate. One should strive for an HR increase of about 15-20 beats/min from one stage to the next.

From the course of the HR speed and pedalling rate curves (Fig. 21), it can be seen that the HR remains at the same accepted level at each stage while speed and pedalling rate are dependent on external influences. The heart rate increases an average 15 beats/min from one stage to the next.
    This is coupled to an increase in speed of about 2 km/h. The average pedalling rate increases to 100 r.p.m. in the last stage. The lactate concentration reaches 8.73 mmol/l. For this cycling field test an integrated cycle computer with additional heart rate measurement ("Cyclovantage" from Polar Sport) is used. The test can also be carried out with the "Sport Tester".

Running Field Test
In the running field test it is recommended to control the stages of intensity via the pace. In the first stage the pace is in the aerobic region at about 75% of average 10

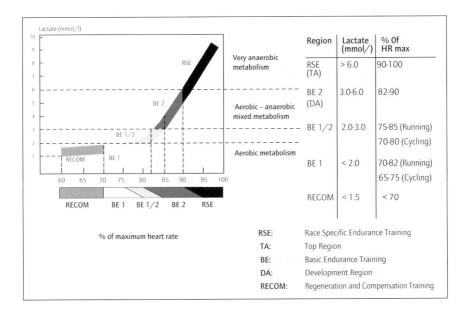

Fig. 20: *Lactate-heart rate diagram and the regions of intensity derived from it for duathlon*

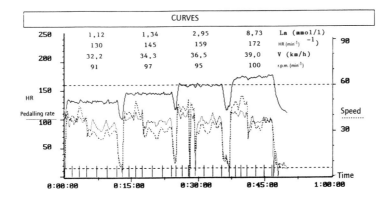

Fig. 21: *Cycling field test over 4 x 6 km: time progression of heart rate, speed and pedalling frequency in the individual stages of exertion of a performance athlete*

km running speed. With every stage there is an increase in speed of 5-10%. As in the cycling field test running speed, lactate concentration and heart rate per stage are measured and related to each other in the lactate/heart rate/speed curve.

7.2.3 Factors Influencing the Lactate Concentration

In the past the biological influences on the blood lactate level were frequently underestimated. A number of scientists have proven that the development of lactate must not be seen only as an aspect of anaerobic muscle metabolism but that further biochemical aspects must also be taken into consideration. For instance, the amount of lactate developed during muscular activity depends to a decisive degree on the amount of glycogen available. If the glycogen stores in the muscles and liver are not sufficiently full, very little lactate can be formed.

At the same performance level this would cause the curve in the lactate-speed diagram to move to the right. In this case the shift falsely represents an improvement in aerobic performance capacity in the aerobic-anaerobic transitional region (2-6 mmol/l). If the glycogen impoverishment is not recognised when evaluating the test results, intensities of exertion that are too high will be set when regulating training load, leading to overtaxing of the athlete.

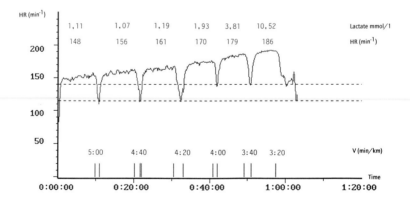

Fig. 22: *Running field test over 6 X 200 m of a duathlete with a 10 km best time of 32:28 minutes.*

The daily routine, sweat production and diet also influence lactate behaviour during muscular activity. If for example energy drinks are drunk before and during the test, the lactate values can be higher than if only water had been drunk.

Regular Monitoring of Intensity of Effort
Because of these influencing factors which cannot always be determined exactly, it is advisable to monitor intensity during training and to ascertain that training is actually taking place in the chosen training region. Using the new fast lactate measuring device athletes can do this themselves by placing themselves under the chosen strain for about 15 minutes and then interrupting their programme and measuring the lactate values.

8 Coupled Training

Coupled training is a special training form in duathlon whereby different endurance disciplines are coupled within one training session. The objective of coupled training is to achieve fast adjustment of the function systems to the new form of movement. In this respect one could call it adjustment training, for the muscles in particular must be "empowered" to adjust to the change in work conditions in a very brief time without major performance loss. Coupled training not only adds variety to duathlon training, it also has a marked influence on race performance.

When running and cycling, athletes carry out movements which are continually repeated. These are so-called automated movement processes whose patterns of movement are relatively constant. If differing movement automatisms are coupled with one another as in duathlon, the changeover from cycling to running can cause adjustment problems, regardless of how good the athlete is. A survey of 30 squad triathletes showed that about half of them had adjustment difficulties in races, especially changing from cycling to running. "It's like running on eggs" is one of the most frequently heard comments on the running feeling after cycling. Not until after the first 1,000 m would they notice an improved running feeling. Fig. 23 shows the main results of the survey.

These adjustment problems can be expressed in the form of a bad running style which can lead to considerable loss of speed in races. Typical examples are not enough stretching at the hips, a "sitting" running posture and flat, short stride.

Race performance is therefore not just the simple addition of the individual performances in running and cycling. With regard to performance structure it is the integration of mutually influencing and interdependent cycling, running and changeover performances. This fact must be taken into account in training structure by using specific coupled training.

Content of Coupled Training

To date no definitely confirmed methodology has been extrapolated from the small number of studies on coupled training. It is, however, recommended to rigorously incorporate coupled training in the annual training process. The proportion of total training should be about 25%.

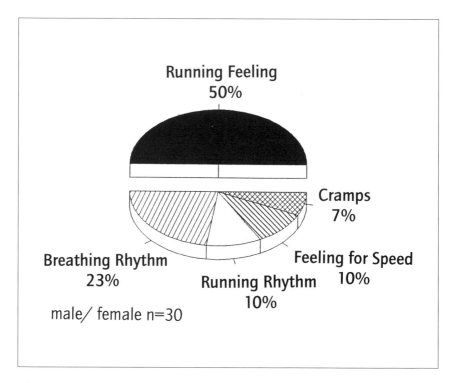

Fig. 23: Adjustment problems after the changeover from cycling to running in triathlon races. Results of a survey of 30 squad triathletes (from PFÜTZNER et al. 1994, 112)

In the individual periods coupled training has main points of emphasis in relationship to the principles of physical effort. In the general preparatory period, semi-specific forms of coupling (cross-country skiing/running) are chosen; in the special preparatory period special forms; and in the race period race specific coupling forms. Here are some examples of coupled training in the individual periods.

Semi-specific Coupled Training (Preparatory Period I and II)

Objective: Create basic performance prerequisites for the coupling of differing forms of endurance strain

RUN & BIKE, a semi-specific form of coupled training

Example 1: Cross-country Skiing (Rollskis) & RECOM Running

Before or after cross-country ski training, or rollski training, a slow jog in the RECOM region is carried out for a period under 45 minutes.

Example 2: RUN & BIKE

RUN & BIKE is an organised form of endurance training in which two people cover a certain distance together as a team, on a bike and running. One partner runs while the other cycles. They can change as often and at any time they want. The bike is given from partner to partner. The demands on the athletes depend very much on the terrain. If it is rough, the running activity is exerting, while the cycling becomes a RECOM ride. When the *total duration of effort* is over three hours the *intensity* of this should be in the BE 1 region, if two to three hours in BE 1/2 and if shorter still the running or cycling can be carried out in the BE 2 or even in the RSE region. RUN & BIKE in the region of higher intensity should not be done before preparatory period III.

Run & Bike

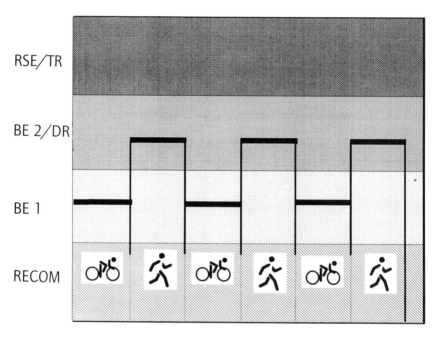

Duration of effort (2-4 h)
Change of activity every 10-20 min

Fig. 24: RUN & BIKE (from HOTTENROTT/ZÜLCH 1995)

Example 3: MTB Fartlek (BE 1/2) and medium, extensive Jogging (BE 1)

"MTB (mountain bike) fartlek" is carried out according to the alternating duration method on easy to medium profile terrain. According to the route, athletes "play" with the speed and the pedalling frequency. The intensity of effort is in the aerobic-anaerobic transitional region (BE 1/2).

The duration overall should be at least an hour and at the most three hours. The following medium extensive jog is run in BE 1 for 45 to 90 min using the continuous duration method.

Example 4: Intensive MTB Hill Climb (SE 2) and long, extensive Jogging (BE 1)

Ride the mountain bike intensively on a strong profile hill section of 20-40 km. This is followed by a long, extensive fat metabolism run of at least 90 min in the lower BE 1 region.

It is also possible to use a rolling machine or road bike for training. If using the rolling machine the extensive interval method should be used.

Here are two examples of this:
a) 4-6 x 5 min with 5 min active break
b) 3-5 x 10 min with 5 min active break
Pedalling rate should be between 70 and 80 r.p.m.

Specific Coupled Training (Preparatory Period II and III)

Objective: Create special performance prerequisites for the coupling of running and cycling

Example 5: Long extensive cycling (BE 1) and fast jogging (BE 2)

A long, extensive cycling ride of three hours in BE 1 is coupled with fast jogging (BE 2) over 2 to 6 km. The training session ends after easy cool down running of at least ten minutes followed by stretching.

Example 6: Short, intensive cycling (BE 2) and fast jogging (BE 2) and short, intensive cycling (BE 2)

The coupling session is done in BE 2 and consists of two short, intensive cycling components over 15 to 30 km with a fast jog over 3-8 km in between. On short sections of the course, cycling and running can be coupled with one another several times (3-5 times).

Example 7: Fast jogging (BE 2) and short, intensive cycling (BE 2) and fast jogging (BE 2)

A fast jog of 3-6 km is followed by a short, intensive cycling session over 15 to 30 km and a second fast jog over 3-8 km.

All three components are done according to the continuous duration method in BE 2. On short sections of the course cycling and running can be coupled with one another several times (3-5 times).

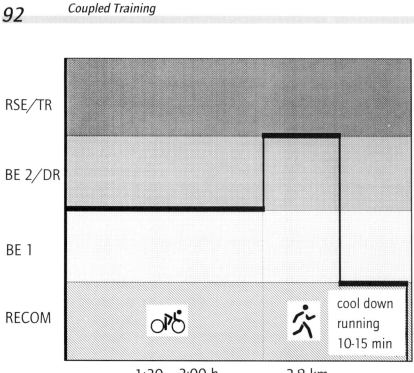

RSE/TR

BE 2/DR

BE 1

RECOM

cool down
running
10-15 min

1:30 – 3:00 h   3-8 km

Fig. 25: Coupled training: after a long, extensive cycling session a fast jog is carried out (from HOTTENROTT/ZÜLCH 1995).

Race Specific Coupled Training (Race Period)

Objective: Create race specific coupling abilities for running and cycling

Example 8: Fast running (RSE) and medium to long, extensive cycling (BE 1)
After a warm-up run (15-20 min) a fast run at race speed over 2 to 6 km is coupled with a medium to long, extensive cycling session over 40 to 100 km.

Example 9: Race cycling (RSE) and medium to long jogging (BE 1)
After warm-up cycling (20-30 min) a distance of 10-30 km is covered at race specific speed. Without a break this is followed by a medium to long, extensive jog of 45 to 90 minutes.

Example 10: Multi-coupling: Fast run (RSE) and fast cycling (RSE)

After a warm-up run (15-20 min) a fast run over 1 to 3 km is coupled with a fast cycling session over 3 to 10 km two to four times without a break. After the last coupling the training session ends with easy cool down cycling.

Example 11: Duathlon to check performance (RSE)

As preparation for racing, and a check on performance, a duathlon is carried out almost at race speed on a measured route over a shorter distance. To analyse performance the split times and the heart rate readings are recorded. In performance and high performance athletics the lactate reading after each partial discipline can also be ascertained. Short-distance duathletes choose a running distance of 3-4 km and a cycling distance of 20-25 km, long-distance duathletes cover roughly twice that.

Performance Check Duathlon (RSE)

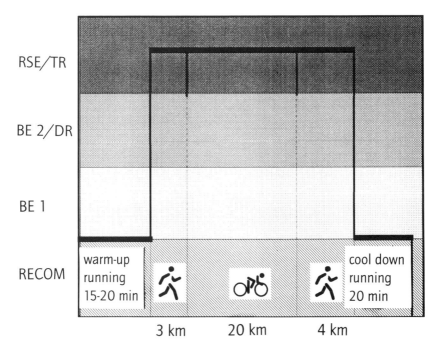

Fig. 26: Duathlon to check performance (from HOTTENROTT/ZÜLCH 1995)

In coupled training, particular attention must be paid to running. The reason is that straight after cycling the movement structure in running is different to what it is normally. It is therefore advisable to do targeted running training in the transitional phase. The emphasis should be on conscious stretching of the hips and pulling during the supporting phase to create horizontal speed. Additionally, coupled training shortens the periods of adjustment to the various movement structures. This contributes to maintaining high performance capacity on the running section.

Tips for the Race

In order to adjust quickly to the new form of movement, BREMER (1991, 145) suggests using the phases of the cycling race when it is not absolutely necessary to pedal, i.e. downhill sections, to stretch the back leg extensor muscles (ischiocrural muscles) when the pedal is down by lowering the heel. The author's own research has shown that this should not be done just before the cycling section ends because running calls for a shorter working length of the ischiocrural muscles, and stretching thus works contra-indicatively for the running that follows. Stretching just before the cycling finishes increases the length of the ischiocrurals. This leads to longer strides at the beginning of the run which in turn disturbs the running rhythm and can lead to reduction in speed.

It has proven useful to cycle the last kilometres before the changeover using a lower gear and higher pedalling rate. Increasing pedalling rate leads to increased muscle tone which can have a favourable effect on regulating the necessary muscle working length required for running.

Seen biomechanically, the loosening of the muscles through increasing frequency while cycling, assumed by a number of authors, cannot take place because an increase in frequency means an increase in muscle tone and an increase in static strain. An increase in the activity of the dynamic proportion can on the other hand be achieved through increased resistance (MÜLLER et al. 1989, 24).

The author's own research on muscle activity also showed that the ischiocrural muscles, which are responsible for stretching at the hip and pulling in the supporting phase, have the effect of limiting performance during races when muscle tiring sets in. Therefore it is necessary to provide additional strength training for these muscles, which can decisively influence speed in cycling and in running (see chapter 11).

9 Building up Performance over Several Years

World class performance in sport is only achievable when talents are discovered as early as possible and steadfastly supported. Only when performance and training are effectively given direction at an early stage, that is, only when training methods and measures are structured with a performance orientation right from the start, can top performances be achieved. This also applies to duathlon. Here too training must be built up systematically from childhood and youth in order to achieve performance at the highest level in adult competition.

Such a long-term training concept brings up a number of questions of course. For example, the performance prerequisites in duathlon today are based on current experience and knowledge. With regard to future world class performance it is necessary, however, to view training in perspective, not to orient it to current but to future top performance. Equally decisive in the framework of long-term training planning is the age at which performance in running and cycling reaches a peak, which must be kept in mind if the biological performance peak is not to be missed. Finally, it is essential to structure training effectively over the years so that training and demands lead to optimal performance improvement for the individual athlete.

In duathlon we can identify five training sectors for long-term development of performance:

9.1 Basic Education (Child Training)

In addition to gaining general and all-round motor abilities and skills, children up to about 14 years of age should become familiar with varied running and cycling training, whereby the training sessions and distances should not be too long. Participation in children's duathlons is recommended. It gives added motivation to training and requires no special preparation. At this age the playful character of sport should always be in the foreground.

In children's duathlon it is important to ensure a traffic free and relatively flat course.

9.2 Basic Training (Youth Training I)

Young people aged between about 15 and 16 should develop their general and sport specific performance. A well-developed state of all-round sporting performance capability, together with an increase in the capacity of the physical structure should be achieved, and motor abilities in cycling and running should be harmonised and economised. Additionally duathlon specific performance motivation for training and races should be achieved.

9.3 Further Training (Youth Training II)

In this training sector, ususally completed between the ages of 17 and 18, one should not concentrate on general sports training, but rather on the sport specific development of performance capacity. In this phase the foundations should be laid for the long-term development of performance in duathlon. Long-term fitness in cycling and running can be increased up to training over longer distances than required, in order to achieve higher aerobic capacity. Regarding technique, attention should be paid to the development of the best form.

9.4 Additional Training (Junior Training)

When aged between 19 and 20, athletes who have achieved the objectives of the previous sectors can follow this with a training phase of at least two years which is designed to qualify them for training and competing in the high performance field. Accordingly this is characterised by more targeted training measures in all regions. The proportion of special, intensive and race-like training increases. The training structure, means and methods are oriented towards the A and B squads.

9.5 High Performance Training (Adult Training)

High performance training assumes that junior training has been successfully completed. Top international performances are rarely achieved before the age of 21. The ages mentioned here are of course a guide only. The objectives of the particular training sectors may be achieved earlier or later, depending on the individual. If, for example, an athlete with little training sets himself the goal of taking part in the Powerman Duathlon Zofingen, he would have to go through a three to five year training build-up, depending on his talent. If the person is a particularly talented early

Successful young duathlete Holger Rohde (3rd in the German Junior Championships)

developer, or has endurance experience from other sports, or built up a great deal of endurance capability during childhood, the objective might be achieved sooner. Generally though, as a result of physical growth and adaptive processes, set-backs must be expected even within a constantly carried out programme of performance development.

Many amateur athletes wish to participate in top events after only a relatively short period of training. This is not always without risk from a health point of view. Endurance capacity cannot be developed over night, the body always follows the

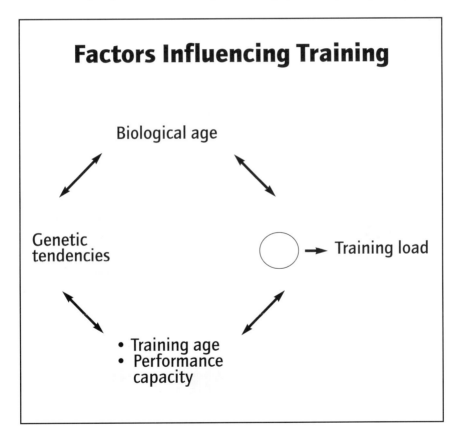

Fig. 27: Relationship between genetic tendencies, biological age, training age and training load (from MARTIN 1988, 31)

rules of adaptation. This has been covered extensively in chapter 5. When structuring training for young people, it is imperative that the following principles are adhered to:

1.   In contrast to adult training, for adolescents the stage of biological development determines what can be trained, how often and at what intensity.

2.   Young people's current state of development and performance capacity must be constantly monitored and the training load adjusted accordingly.

3.   Biological age, training age, performance capacity and genetic tendencies must all be taken into consideration when determining the amount of effort demanded (Fig. 27).

4.   In build-up training the principle of gradualness applies.

Table 10 illustrates a long-term build-up of performance capacity from youth to adulthood.

Table 10: Long-term build-up of performance capacity in duathlon

Age (Years)	Athletics h/year	Cycling km/year	Running km/year	Amount h/year	Amount h/week
15	100	3,000	1,200	300	6
16	100	4,000	1,600	350	8
17	100	5,000	2,000	440	10
18	100	6,000	2,500	530	12
19	100	7,000	3,000	620	14
20	100	9,000	3,500	750	17
21	100	12,000	4,000	850	20
22	100	15,000	4,500	1,000	24

In the field of triathlon/duathlon Normann Stadler is an exceptional example of a developmentally sound and long-term oriented approach to top performance. At 14 he was selected for the triathlon C squad and systematically trained. In the youth categories he was German Triathlon Champion four times in a row. As a junior he reached 3rd place in the Duathlon World Championships in Frankfurt, and in the main class he became European vice-champion at age 22 in the spring of 1994 and in autumn of the same year he was world champion in duathlon.

The amount of training done by Normann Stadler as a youth and a junior was much less than that of other squad athletes. His training in younger years was highly geared to quality. Throughout the year training sessions to improve running and cycling technique, speed and stretching and strengthening of the muscles were integrated in the weekly programme. The athlete developed an extremely economical running and cycling technique, which at the same time provided the best prerequisites for the amount and strength of the training that followed.

Normann Stadler: most successful triathlete in his youth and duathlon world champion in 1994

Training Report

Day	Time	Type	km	min	Training content	Method	subj. strain	TPF	RPF
Mon	11:30	Game		90	Volleyball/School	Game	3		52
	17:00	R	4	35	Technique/Running order	Technique	2		
	17:45	R	4.5	25	mJ, Running style	mJ	3	135	
Tue	16:45	S	2.1	65	400 m warm-up, 10 x 50 over 50", 200 rounds, 10 x 50 cool down	I	3-4	180	54
	19:45	C	8	20	high frequency, low gears (loosening up)	SEC	2	130	
Wed	17:00	R	11.5	70	2 x 5km (19:10, 18:20) Stretching, 1.5 km cool	fJ	3	185	54
	19:00	Other		30	down, gymnastics				
Thu	17:10	S	2.2	60	400 m warm-up, 1,000 (14:32) 200 rounds, 400 pace change, 200 cool down	fES, speed play	4-5	175	52
	18:10	Other		15	Stretching				
Fri	17:30	C	16	35	High freq., low gears	mEC	3	135	52
	18:15	Other		20	Fitness gymnastics				
Sat	11:10	S	2.1	60	400 m warm-up, 5 x 50 in betw. 200 easy 10 x 50 pace change, 300 cool down	I, F	4-5	175	56
	16:55	R	11	47	Cross-country	F	2-3		
Sun	11:05	R	9.7	36	Fast pace, head winds	fJ	4	185	48
	11:45	Other		15	Stretching				

Total	TS	km	min	Notes	Weight:	67.5 kg
Swimming	3	6.4	185	Emphasis:		
Cycling	2	24	55	Running technique		
Running	4	37.7	198			
Other	6		185		Total:	10 h *23 min*

Key: R: Running, S: Swimming, C: Cycling, mJ: medium jogging, SEC: slow endurance cycling, fJ: fast jogging, fES: fast endurance swimming, mEC: medium endurance cycling, I: interval method, F: Fartlek

Table 11: Typical training week in Normann Stadlers preparatory period I at the age of 16 years

Table 12: Training report of Normann Stadler at the age of 18 years, two weeks before the European Triathlon Championships in Losheim in which he attained 2nd place in the youth section. Best times 1991: 1,500 m swimming (25 m length): 20:25 min; 40 km (individual times): 55 min; 5,000 m (track) 16:03 min; 10,000 m (road): 32:30 min

Training Report

Day	Time	Type	km	min	Training content	Method	subj. strain	TPF	RPF
Mon	10:00 15:00	R C Other	15 90	70 140 20	On forest floor Flat course Stretching	mJ mEC	3 3	135 130	
Tue	16:30 18:00	S R Other	4 20	85 100 20	With neo in lake Flat asphalt course Stretching	mES mJ	3	130	44
We	16:15 19:20	C S Other	11,5	70 30	10 km uphill (calmly) With neo in lake Stretching	fEC sES	4 5	160- 180	
Thu	17:00	R Other	10	60 20	6 x 1,000m in 3:30 min Stretching	I	4	-190	50
Fri	16:20 19:00	C R Other	75 10	140 40 10	Rough course Fartlek Stretching	F I	4 3	-155 -175	48
Sat	11:00 12:15	S C Other	3,2 55	60 90 20	W.o. break in lake Stretching	sES sEC	3 1	120	50
Sun	10:15	C R Other	52 5	90 < 17 20	Cycled uphill Followed by fast run Stretching	mJ fJ	2-3 5	-140 185	42

Total	TS	km	min	Notes	Weight:
Swimming	3	9,2	185	* Was totally worn out!	
Cycling	5	312	530		
Running	5	60	290	Emphasis:	
Other	7		130	Large amount of training	**Total:** 18 h *55 min*

*neo = neoprane wetsuit

Training Amounts of a Successful Triathlete

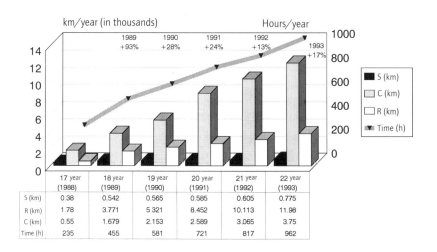

	17 year (1988)	18 year (1989)	19 year (1990)	20 year (1991)	21 year (1992)	22 year (1993)
S (km)	0.38	0.542	0.565	0.585	0.605	0.775
R (km)	1.78	3.771	5.321	8.452	10.113	11.98
C (km)	0.55	1.679	2.153	2.589	3.065	3.75
Time (h)	235	455	581	721	817	962

Fig. 28: Training figures of a successful young triathlete over six years

To give an idea of the relationship between training and performance during a long-term build-up of performance, the training and performance figures of a successful young triathlete over a period of six years are shown here (Fig. 28).

Fig. 28 gives an overview of the annual amount of training in swimming, cycling and running in each of six training years. The amount of training increases annually by 13% to 93%, whereby the growth rates decrease up until the 5th year and increase again in the 6th year.

With this amount of training the athlete was placed 3rd in the junior class of the German Championships in his 3rd training year (1990). In the 5th and 6th year he was placed 6th and 8th in the main men's class.

Cycling Performance

His cycling fitness was determined annually in the competition season on the cycle ergometer (beginning at 100 Watt, increasing by 10 Watt every 30 s). Using the lactate performance curve, endurance ability can easily be ascertained.

Development of Performance in Cycling

Lactate Performance Curves

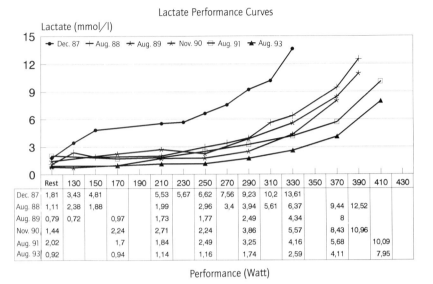

	Rest	130	150	170	190	210	230	250	270	290	310	330	350	370	390	410	430
Dec. 87	1,81	3,43	4,81			5,53	5,67	6,62	7,56	9,23	10,2	13,61					
Aug. 88	1,11	2,38	1,88			1,99		2,96	3,4	3,94	5,61	6,37		9,44	12,52		
Aug. 89	0,79	0,72		0,97		1,73		1,77		2,49		4,34		8			
Nov. 90	1,44			2,24		2,71		2,24		3,86		5,57		8,43	10,96		
Aug. 91	2,02			1,7		1,84		2,49		3,25		4,16		5,68		10,09	
Aug. 93	0,92			0,94		1,14		1,16		1,74		2,59		4,11		7,95	

Performance (Watt)

Fig. 29: Development of a triathletes cycling performance over six years, shown using the lactate performance curves of the cycle ergometer staged test.

If the curve moves to the right it means that at the same level of performance less lactate is created.

This is caused by increased aerobic use of energy. After the 1st training year a particularly pronounced move to the right can be seen. At a lactate concentration of 6 mmol/l performance increases from 240 Watt to 320 Watt (+ 33%) and at 3 mmol/l from 125 Watt to 250 Watt (+ 100%).

In the following years performance capacity continues to increase in the anaerobic transitional region. In the 6th year, at 6 mmol/l lactate it is 385 Watt (increase over starting value of 60%) and at 3 mmol/l lactate it is 340 Watt (increase of 172%).

In terms of absolute performance the growth rates are lower. After six training years the starting value of 330 Watt increases by 25% to 410 Watt. In the same period the maximum lactate concentration decreases from 13.61 mmol/l to 7.95 mmol/l (-58%).

Development of Performance in Running

Conconi Test

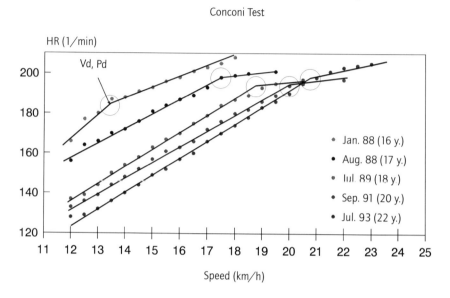

Fig. 30: Development of the running performance of a triathlete over six years, shown using the heart rate-speed curves of the Conconi test.

Running Performance

The development of performance in running is explained using the results of the Conconi test. Moves to the right of the heart rate-speed curves can be identified. At the same speed the heart rate sinks. Over the years the aerobic proportion continues to increase, while the aerobic-anaerobic proportion decreases in relationship to overall performance. The speed at the point of deflection increases from 13.5 km/h in the 1st year to 19.3 km/h in the 6th year. This represents increased performance of 26%.

This example shows very clearly the relationship between training effort and increased performance. Whereas in the first training years the athlete achieves high performance growth with relatively few hours of training, in the high performance field more than 1,000 hours per year are required for a much smaller increase in performance. A weekly training volume of 25-40 hours is realistic for top athletes.

Anyone considering going for top performance in sport should ask themselves at an early stage whether they are prepared to neglect other important aspects of their lives in favour of performance sport. It should be clear to them that a sporting career has many ups and downs and often ends suddenly through unfortunate circumstances. It may happen that many years of training and all the sacrifices that went with it later seem to have been a waste of time.

Requirements of a Long-Term Training Build-up

The efforts of trainers and coaches should not be solely directed at applying what are thought to be the best training methods in order to optimise performance, rather the entire personal development of the athlete should always be supported. If you decide to train according to the objectives shown (table 10), you must be aware that pushing into high performance often has side effects. The athlete's health is the most important objective.

Therefore the health risk must remain calculable. Regular health checks, preventative measures aimed at known weak points and early diagnosis are absolutely essential elements of the path to performance sport through a long-term training build-up.

10 Intelligent Planning and Training

10.1 Training Planning – Foundation for Successful Training

At the beginning of every season athletes and trainers must occupy themselves with planning training. The basics of training planning were discussed in chapter 5. Here we will look at actually planning training. One of the first steps is to analyse the previous year's races and training, as well as the personal and environmental prerequisites for training. A critical judgement of the previous training period is the foundation for deciding the training objectives, content and methods for the coming season. Regular race analyses help estimate the effectiveness of the training done. This in turn allows one to take appropriate measures regarding the training that follows (see ch. 13).

Following the principle of constantly increasing the load in a long-term performance build-up, an increase in the amount of training should be planned for the coming year. Whereas the beginner can still double the load in the first years, performance athletes can only increase it by 20-40%, and high performance athletes by less than 20%, per year.

Once the athlete has taken these factors into account and determined his amount of training for the year, he can start organising training in a way that fits in with elements of his social environment such as family and work.

After the analysis of the current situation and the determining of training and performance targets for the new season, the main and preparatory races are chosen from the race calendar. In the course of the year one should concentrate on a maximum of 3-5 main races. The number and the dates of the races directly affect the programme of training, which must be taken into consideration when drafting the annual training plan.

10.2 Training Cycle – Planning Work and Recovery

A training cycle describes a target and task-related training period of several months (macro cycle), 2 to 4 weeks (meso cycle) or 2 to 10 days (micro cycle), whereby as a rule weekly and micro cycles are used. After every cycle of work there follows a period

Training Planning

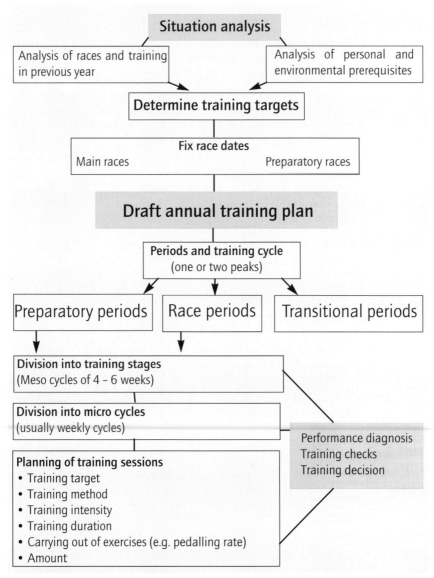

Fig. 31: Training planning procedure

of relief from the strain. The following cycle then begins at a higher level. The duration of a cycle is dependent on the athlete's ability to handle stress. High performance athletes can choose longer cycles than performance and hobby athletes. In endurance performance sport a 2:1 and a 3:1 cycle have proved beneficial, i.e. two to three days (weeks) of increasing followed by a day (or week) of reduced training. For young athletes the 2:1 cycle should be applied.

In the relief phase (recovery) the body should be given enough time to process the training stimuli.

To reach a particular training target it is necessary to go through the micro cycles several times in the course of one meso cycle (training block). This intensifies the directional effect and stabilises performance at a higher level. After a training block of several micro cycles a relief phase of several days is required.

The content of the micro cycle is always dependent on the targets and tasks set for the preparatory period.

10.3 Periodisation – Top Form on Race Day

Periodisation is the term used for the division of the training year into periods with the objective of developing sporting fitness. In other words, periodisation steers towards top condition on race day.

Depending on the objectives and the dates of the races this development can be carried out through simple (the year's preparation aims at a single highlight), double or multiple periodisation. For duathlon a double periodisation is recommended because the race highlights are in spring and autumn.

Double Periodisation

The training year is divided into two macro cycles with several preparatory periods, two race periods and two transitional periods. The training measures aimed at the first annual highlight (spring) begin after a three week transitional period at about the end of October and end in May in week 21 (Duathlon in Zofingen). Training for the second annual highlight (autumn) begins in July and finishes with the last races in late October.

In the three preparatory periods training goes from general to specific with increasing loads. During the race periods the objective is to stabilise performance (Fig. 32). The training periods must be very finely tuned to the races to avoid drops in performance.

Top condition on race day

Table 13: Double Periodisation in Duathlon

Period	Month	Week	Duration
1st Macro cycle			
Preparatory period I	Nov-Dec	45-52	8 wk
Preparatory period II	Jan-Feb	01-08	8 wk
Preparatory period III	March	09-13	5 wk
Race period I	Apr-May	14-21	8 wk
Transitional period	June	22-24	3 wk
2nd Macro cycle			
Preparatory period IV	Jun-Jul	25-29	5 wk
Preparatory period V	August	30-34	5 wk
Race period II	Sep-Oct	35-41	7 wk
Transitional period II	Oct-Nov	42-44	3 wk

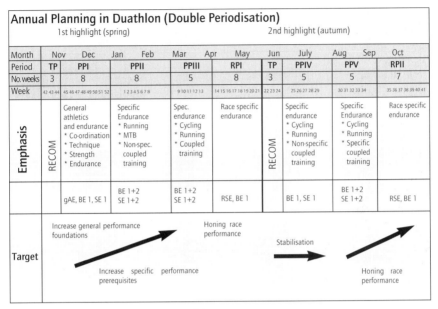

Fig. 32: Double periodisation in duathlon

10.4 Training Proportions of BE, SSE and RSE Training

10.4.1 In the Course of the Year

Determining the proportions of training, i.e. dividing the total training process into percentages of individual training regions, is one of the most difficult parts of planning training.

It is not possible to make generally valid statements on this. The proportions vary from sport to sport and are mainly determined by the athlete's individual situation (structure of muscle fibre), his current performance capacity, the training period and stage and the corresponding amounts of training.

As an example, the proportions of RECOM, BE and RSE training in the course of a year for cycling and running are shown here (Fig. 33 a and b). In the preparatory periods the emphasis of the training measures is on the development of basic endurance capacity. Here BE 1 training plays a dominant role. In running, BE 1 training decreases as a percentage from 70% to 55% from PPI to PPIII. In cycling the percentage of BE 1 stays approximately the same, whereby the absolute number of kilometres cycled rises considerably.

In the race period the proportion of RSE and RECOM training increases, i.e. training is more often at higher intensities and also more often in the RECOM region. The amount of training is lower than in PPIII. In the transitional period the idea is to

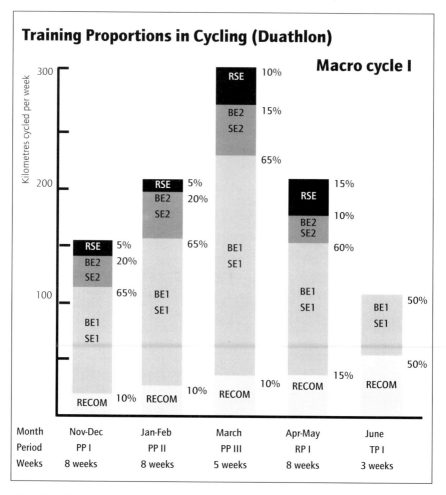

Fig. 33 a: Training proportions in cycling

recover from the strains of racing. A lower dosage of training is important here. Additionally compensational training is done in another sport. The development of basic endurance capacity is always at the beginning of a season, the development of race specific endurance comes directly before and during the race period. Nevertheless, no training regions should be completely neglected during a period. All abilities to be developed should therefore be trained in varying proportions right through the year.

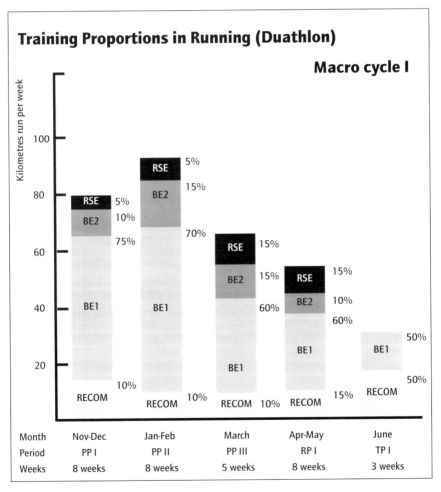

Fig. 33 b: Training proportions in running

10.4.2 In Hoppy, Performance and High Performance Fields

The training proportions do not only change in the course of the year, they are also dependent on the athlete's performance capacity and talent. Fixed recommendations for individual athletes cannot be given here either. It is only possible to provide general guideline values for the relationship of the training regions for hobby, performance and high performance athletes (Fig. 34).

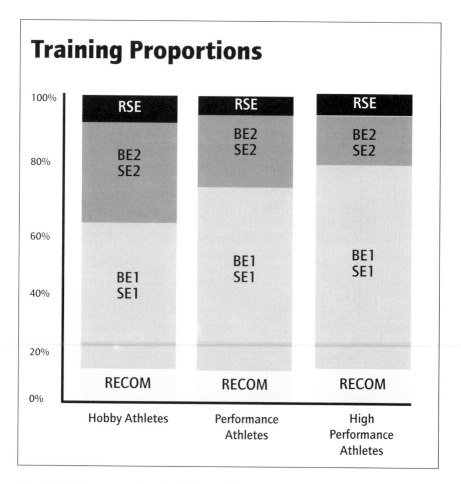

Fig. 34: Training proportions for hobby, performance and high performance athletes

10.5 Training Structure for Ambitious Athletes

The following sections discuss training structure for ambitious athletes using typical weekly cycles in the preparatory and race periods. Column graphs have been chosen to emphasise clearly the basic structures and training principles of a weekly cycle. The height of the column reflects the degree of effort with regard to duration and intensity of the training session. Thus an extensive BE 1 training session lasting several hours can for example have just as high a degree of effort as a short, highly intensive race training (RSE). By using this form, athletes of varying performance capacity can profit from the programme examples. Athletes must determine the amount or duration of a training session themselves according to their performance capacity and the amount of training time per week available to them. It is important that the underlying structure is adhered to even if days off are included, or several sessions are done on one day.

10.5.1 Training in the Preparatory Periods

The training objective in the preparatory periods is to create basic and specific performance prerequisites to reach top condition.

After the transitional period training is gradually stepped up again. The new start should involve no more than 2/3 the amount of training done when the race period ended in October. All those who regulate their training using heart rate or speed coefficients will need to re-determine their individual values. After the transitional period the intensity regions have changed to varying degrees. For duathletes with higher ambitions it is recommended to have a performance diagnostic examination carried out after about a one or two week acclimatisation period in order to determine exactly their fitness and lay down the basic determinants for training. After this they can begin systematic training.

The aim of preparatory period I (PP I) is to create the underlying prerequisites for performance. This is achieved through athletic, strength and basic endurance training. These variations in effort call for a sensible spread of the training sessions over a weekly cycle (Fig. 35). From the point of view of content, the athletics training should be diverse and geared towards the development of co-ordination and form. Exercises in running co-ordination (see table 1, page 25) are well-suited for improving running style. Chapter 11 explains how to put the strength training together. In addition to general strengthening exercises, the emphasis should be on maximum strength training and semi-specific strength endurance training. Every week at least one session of semi-specific coupled training should be included (cf. chapter 8). In running the development of basic endurance ability receives the main attention. After two to three training weeks with increasing intensity a week of regeneration follows.

The aim of preparatory period II is to create specific performance foundations. For this, general athletics training is reduced, strength training to build up the cycling muscles is increased and in running increased basic training is carried out. The total load increases. The training week is divided into two strain blocks of two or three days each. After each training peak a day of regenerative, or compensatory measures, follows in order to re-establish performance capacity and avoid overtaxing. As in PP I a regenerative week follows after two to three training weeks. In the weekly cycle shown here the emphasis is on developing running performance. If the prerequisites are right it is advisable to place a two to three week training emphasis on the development of cycling performance in PP II.

The aim of preparatory period III (PP III) is to create race specific performance foundations. At the beginning of this period the development of basic endurance in cycling should be focused on, for example, a cycling training camp (cf. chapter 15). If basic endurance capability is sufficient, intensive cycling training in the BE 2 and RSE regions can be commenced. In doing so the strength and endurance ability developed should be effectively transferred to the development of race specific speed.

Running training is increasingly tailored to the performance structure of duathlon. Specific coupled training (cf. chapter 8) plays a major part in the weekly programme.

Training in PP IV (July) corresponds roughly to the training measures in PP II, and training in PP V can follow the content of PP III.

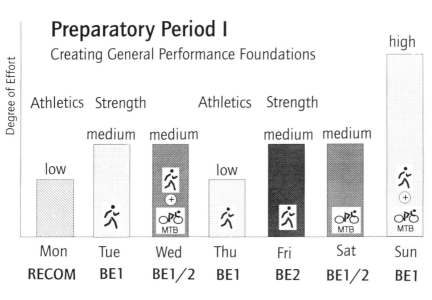

Fig. 35: Weekly cycle in preparatory period I (Nov-Dec)

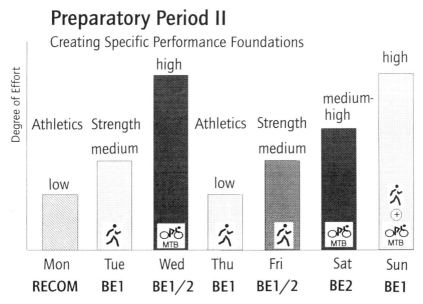

Fig. 36: Weekly cycle in preparatory period II (Jan-Feb)

Preparatory Period III

Creating Race Specific Performance Foundations

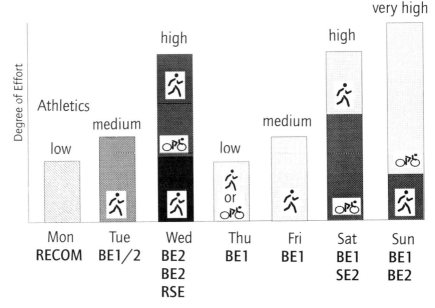

Fig. 37: Weekly cycle in preparatory period III (March)

10.5.2 Training in the Competition Period

A successful competition period is dependent on whether an athlete has managed to use the preparatory periods for large amounts of training in the basic regions in order to achieve   a high capacity for intensive training and racing. Only then can high performance stability throughout the entire competition period be expected. But even a good basic endurance capability can be greatly reduced through overemphasis on highly intensive race specific training, which can in turn lead to instability of performance.

This is especially so when several races are competed in one after the other, for the aerobic performance level has a major role to play in successful placing in several duathlons within a season.

The competition period calls for measures of general and specific race preparation, whereby the latter is referred to as direct race preparation (DRP). It is

Quick changeover during the Powerman Race in Zofingen

Ralph Zeetsen (NL) internationally successful in triathlon and duathlon since his youth

recommended for general preparation of a major race in particular to participate in preparatory races without a tapering phase, i.e. without drastic reductions in training. In this way top performance too early can still be prevented, and the possibility of super compensation of decisive performance foundations for the main race can be kept in reserve.

Direct Preparation of Races (DPR)

By DPR we mean the last period of training (3 to 5 weeks) and the carrying out of special adaptive measures before decisive races.

The aim of DPR is to enable the athlete to optimally transfer to top sporting performance the psychological and physical qualities gained through long-term training.

In order to achieve this there are two interrelated objectives to be worked on in this period:

1. Reaching the greatest possible performance preparedness and performance capacity (top form) on the day of the race.
2. Optimal adaptation to the specific and complex conditions of the race location and routes.

In order to achieve top performance, the correct choice and sequence of training means that the corresponding dynamics of training effort are decisive. In many years of experience in preparing endurance athletes for important races the following division of phases has proven itself:

Recovery Phase – Duration: About One Week

About 4-5 weeks before the main race the athlete has a brief period of active and in particular psychological recovery time lasting about one week. In addition to physiotherapeutic measures the emphasis is on general training elements and cross-training.

Build-Up Phase – Duration: Two to Three Weeks

About 3-4 weeks before the main race there is a build-up phase in which the amount of cycling and running training is increased to a maximum of effort. In the last week sessions of special coupled training are increasingly integrated.

Performance Fine Tuning Phase – Duration: One to Two Weeks

In the last 1-2 weeks before the race the complex sporting performance under specific race conditions is fine tuned. For best adaptation to the race conditions the last training sessions should be carried out at the race location.

In practice it is not always possible to keep to this time framework for DRP. The determination of race dates by commercial interests is having an increasingly disruptive effect on the DRP structure. These force one to go against principles of adaptation and require compromise solutions in race preparation (NEUMANN 1994).

Dietary planning is of special importance in the last week before a major race. A maximum super compensation effect on race day can only be achieved by sensible co-ordination of all measures. A suggestion for training and dietary planning ten days before a duathlon race can be found in chapter 14.4.2 (pa. 177ff.)

A great deal of experience and knowledge is required for the right structuring of training in the competition period. Training before, after, and between the races has varying objectives and roles. With regard to training structure four weekly cycles are differentiated from each other.

Typical Weekly Cycles in the Competition Period

Type 1: Training week
Type 2: Training week after a race
Type 3: Race week
Type 4: Race week after a race

Type 1: Training week

In order to structure training individually between two races the previous training and race loads must be closely analysed (cf. chapter 13). If deficits are discovered, training should be aimed at removing these. The analysis could show, for example, that the athlete was not pushed to the full during the race so that after it he had the feeling he could cover the same distances again. In such a case the amount of training would need to be reduced and the intensity perhaps increased. A favourable combination is the coupling of highly intensive training sessions for the development of great muscular mobilisation ability with extensive training sessions of medium length to stabilise performance. In running, fast runs over 50 to 400 m (e.g. 8 x 300 m with

100 m walking break) and jogs in the BE 1 region over 12-20 km are a good option. The extensive jogs should include a number of accelerations (30 m) and intensity increases (80 m).

If on the other hand good results were achieved in the previous race, training up until the next race has the job of stabilising the standard of performance. In this case the amount and the intensity of training must be reduced. Training in the region of BE 2 should be avoided. Brief amounts of highly intensive training can be included in BE 1 training.

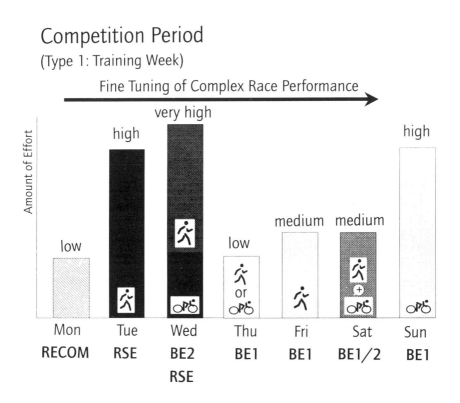

Fig. 38: Weekly cycle in the competition period (Type 1: Training week)

Type 2: Training week after a race

The aim of the training week after a race week is to redevelop performance capacity as quickly as possible and to create favourable performance prerequisites for the following races.

For this the week is divided into two parts. In the first half the emphasis should be on regenerative measures (massages, a warm bath, sleep). Training takes place in the RECOM region, i.e. intensity is very low and the duration of effort is at the most 45 minutes in running and 90 minutes in cycling. A swimming session is also recommended to loosen up and relax the muscles.

In the second half of the week medium amounts and intensities of training are taken up again. A climax should not be aimed for before Saturday.

Competition Period
(Type 2: Training Week After A Race)

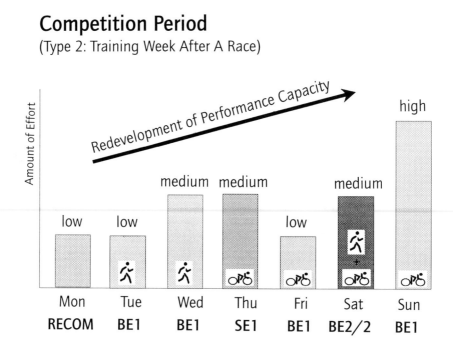

Fig. 39: Weekly cycle in the competition period (Type 2: Training week after a race)

Type 3: Race week

Training for a major race can best be planned when there has been no important race for at least two weeks.

The strain structure of the micro cycle in the race week should be worked out in such a way that an optimal super compensation effect is achieved on race day. To this end the week is divided into two phases. In the first half the amount of effort increases to reach a climax on Wednesday.

Depending on the timing of the race within the seasonal calendar this can be short, race specific or long extensive exertion. If the main race is at the start of the season it is recommended to have race specific training on Wednesday. This could be a short distance duathlon (2.5 km – 20 km – 2.5 km) or a training session using the interval or repetition method. An example of this:

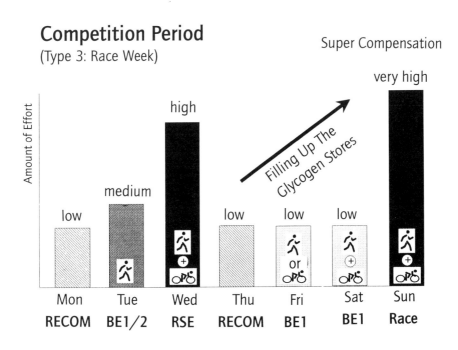

Fig. 40: Weekly cycle in the competition period (Type 3: Race week)

- Cycling (mornings): 4-6 x 5 km at race speed with 10 min active break
- Running (afternoons): 6-10 x 300 m at race speed with 500 m active jogging break.

If on the other hand the main race is at the end of the season and several races have already taken place, it is recommended to place the emphasis on extensive training. An example:

- Cycling (mornings): 60-100 km in the BE1 region with 4-6 accelerations and 4-6 flying sprints over 50 m. Between the intensive, brief motor bursts an active break of at least three minutes should be adhered to.
- Running (afternoons): 8-15 km running in the BE1 region followed by 4-6 intensive interval runs over 300 m with 100 m walking break. 4-6 km cool down in the RECOM region.

Type 4: Race week after a race

In the duathlon competition period the situation often arises that the athlete wishes to compete successfully in races on consecutive weekends. Planning for this requires an emphasis on basic training in the last weeks before the race series. Athletes can only complete several races in a row without loss of performance if a stable performance capacity has been developed.

The various measures between the races are primarily targeted at fast regeneration. The training sessions are characterised by low to medium amounts and intensities which can be diversely structured using accelerations, increases in intensity and sprints.

To achieve the super compensation effect the greatest loads are placed in the middle of the week. The degree of effort is in direct relationship to the regeneration state of the athlete.

With the determination of periodisation and cyclisation the annual planning is more or less complete. Provision should also be made, however, for the planning of performance diagnostic tests and measures to check training at any time during the year in order to be able to make decisions about further training. Sticking rigidly to the annual plan is definitely not recommended. The actual carrying out of the training plan must always be adapted to current performance capacity at any given time.

Competition Period
(Type 4: Race Week after a Race)

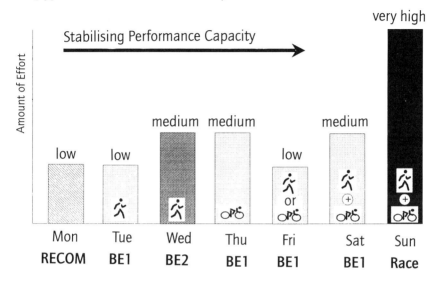

Fig. 41: *Weekly cycle in the competition period (Type 4: Race week after a race)*

10.5.3 Training in the Transitional Period

The aim of the transitional period is to release oneself from race stress and draw motivation, endurance and strength for another training year. Running and cycling training is drastically reduced. Recovery, leisure, switching off and being aware of other things in life are now on the agenda.

Of course for one's own feeling of well-being sports activity should not fall right down to zero, but sport should not be restricted to running and cycling; ball games, raquet games, swimming or hiking with friends are recommended alternatives. Many also use the transitional periods to recover from injuries and have health checks.

During the transitional period nutrition should also receive attention. The considerably lower level of training exertion naturally requires a reduction in daily calorie intake otherwise there will be rapid weight gain. Older athletes in particular (over 40) usually have difficulty reducing body weight after the transitional period.

10.6 Preparing for Race Conditions

Adaptation to a changed day-night rhythm
Duathlon races which do not take place in the European time zone require athletes to change their habitual day-night rhythm. Even with a time difference of five or six hours there can be difficulties in adapting which can last up to five days. It is therefore recommended to travel to the race location early enough (5-7 days before the race starts).

Adaptation to temperature and humidity extremes
The climatic conditions at the race location must also be taken into consideration. Extremely high temperatures and humidity can have negative effects on the performance capacity of those athletes in particular who are not used to such a climate, so in addition to arriving in plenty of time specific measures should be taken during training. These include saunas, toughening measures or training in locations with similar conditions to the race location.

Adaptation to the specific demands of race routes
The specific demands of the race route (profile, course, wind and visibility conditions) should be known early so that these conditions can be simulated as exactly as possible in training. Here too, however, it is recommended to arrive in plenty of time so that athletes can adjust to good advantage to the conditions on the spot.

Adjusting to the general race atmosphere
Inexperienced race athletes in particular should not be sent unprepared to races at which they may find unusual conditions. For instance in some places the behaviour of spectators, judges and the press can differ significantly from the usual picture one has of them.

11 Strength Training

– in Cooperation with Martin Zülch –

11.1 Performance Reserve for all Athletes

The higher the performance capacity of an athlete the more important strength training becomes for further performance improvement in duathlon. On the whole strength training represents a performance reserve for all athletes. In addition to strengthening the muscle groups that work to drive one forward, particular care should be taken to develop strong torso muscles. Having strong muscles in the whole body helps prevent sporting injuries, contributes to good running and cycling technique and thus ensures stable performance capacity during the whole race. If, for example, the torso muscles are too weak, with increasing tiredness this can negatively affect technique.

The torso can then no longer carry out sufficiently its function of "counterpoint" to leg movement.

Strength ability can be most effectively trained through targeted strength training over several weeks using general, semi-specific and specific means. In this context the main aim is to improve strength endurance. Strength endurance is the muscles' resistance to tiring during long-lasting application of strength in which the use of strength is more than 30% of maximum strength. Components of strength endurance determining performance are thus maximum strength and aerobic and anaerobic endurance.

Too great a proportion of maximum strength can negatively affect endurance performance capacity. If, for example, through strength training the muscle diameter increases too much this can lead to an unfavourable burden-strength relationship, restriction of mobility and deterioration of movement coordination and technique.

The aim of duathlon specific strength training is not to develop maximum strength endurance but rather optimal strength endurance oriented towards the specific demands of duathlon racing. Strength endurance training in duathlon is thus first and foremost aerobic and anaerobic endurance training against medium resistance (hill runs, runs with additional weights etc.). This is supported with training on devices for developing maximum strength with the emphasis on improving intra-muscular co-ordination, and with semi-specific strength endurance training.

Optimising intra-muscular coordination (within a muscle) means that more motor units can contract at the same time. The term motor unit describes the number of muscle fibres activated by a motor nerve cell. While an untrained person, despite great effort, can simultaneously contract about 65% of his fibres, a strength trained athlete can use up to 95% of his fibres because the synchronic activation of the available motor units is considerably better (FREY/HILDENBRANDT 1994, 70). Muscle volume only increases marginally or not at all in intra-coordinative maximum strength training (IC training).

11.2 Periodisation in the Course of the Year

There is a lot of uncertainty amongst trainers and athletes about periodisation of strength training in the course of the year.

Correct methodical procedure depends on many factors which must be considered when actually developing a plan. The athlete's reaction to strength training stimuli can vary considerably and is directly linked to the composition of the muscle fibres (proportion of ST and FT fibres) and the hormonal status of the individual.

In order to create high race specific strength endurance capacity, in the course of the year one must begin with the development of a higher strength level. In PP I from November to December the emphasis is on maximum strength training and semi-specific strength endurance training.

In PP II from January to February the amount of both training forms is increased. In PP III when training on machines only strength endurance capacity is trained using semi-specific means.

In the competition period strength training on machines should not be carried out because of the risk of disturbing stimuli affecting the skeletal muscles and aerobic endurance capacity. Specific strength endurance training SE 1 and SE 2 (cf. chapter 6) is integrated in the training process all year round, with accentuation (training camp) in PP III.

In the second macro cycle the same principles are followed. The aim is to use brief addressing of the individual strength abilities in order to redevelop and stabilise the strength developed in the first macro cycle (see Fig. 42).

Periodisation of Strength Training in Duathlon

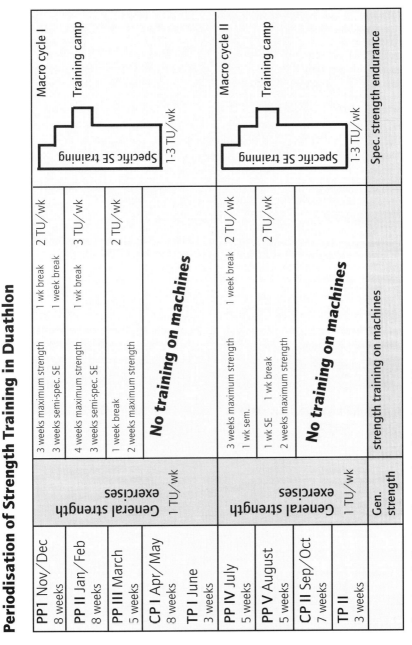

	General strength exercises			Specific SE training
PP1 Nov/Dec 8 weeks	3 weeks maximum strength 3 weeks semi-spec. SE	1 wk break 1 week break	2 TU/wk	Macro cycle I / Training camp
PP II Jan/Feb 8 weeks	4 weeks maximum strength 3 weeks semi-spec. SE	1 wk break	3 TU/wk	
PP III March 5 weeks	1 week break 2 weeks maximum strength		2 TU/wk	
CP I Apr/May 8 weeks	**No training on machines**			1-3 TU/wk
TP I June 3 weeks	1 TU/wk			
PP IV July 5 weeks	3 weeks maximum strength 1 wk sem.	1 week break	2 TU/wk	Macro cycle II / Training camp
PP V August 5 weeks	1 wk SE 2 weeks maximum strength	1 wk break	2 TU/wk	
CP II Sep/Oct 7 weeks	**No training on machines**			1-3 TU/wk
TP II 3 weeks	1 TU/wk			
Gen. strength	strength training on machines			Spec. strength endurance

Fig. 42: Periodisation of strength training in duathlon

11.3 General Strengthening Exercises

General strengthening exercises are a regular component of annual training and should be carried out at least twice a week. The emphasis should be on strengthening the torso. In chapter 4 a number of exercises are recommended.

11.4 Maximum Strength Training

Maximum strength is the greatest possible strength that an athlete can voluntarily exert against resistance. Maximum strength is a performance determining component of strength endurance. Determining maximum strength, using a test in which a great weight is moved once, should not be done because of the risk of injury. In the training process with duathletes it has been found useful to establish intensity using the number of repeats at a certain weight. With beginners one assumes that at an intensity of 50% ten repeats are possible, and these ten should be done in the last series to be trained. 5% more intensity in each case means one repeat less (GROSSER 1989, 60).

Which method for training maximum strength is best in duathlon?
We differentiate between static and dynamic training of maximum strength. The dynamic form is further differentiated in a muscle build-up, or muscle diameter training (MD training), and a training of intra-muscular coordination ability (IC training).

In training practice a combination of MD and IC training has proven itself. Here a weight is chosen which can be quickly moved 10-12 times per series while maintaining optimal moving amplitude. With beginners this is about 50-60%, and with advanced athletes about 60-70% of maximum strain. The weight is put down briefly (< 1 s) after every exertion to relax the muscles. Purely intra-coordinative maximum strength training at a load of over 85% and about 2-6 repeats per series should only be carried out – if at all – by really top athletes.

Strength training is begun in preparatory period I. Initially, twice a week six to eight exercises in two to three series are carried out. When performance capacity is more advanced the programme is carried out three days a week and with more series (4 to 5). The break between series should be two to three minutes long.

The strength training exercise programme is structured in such a way that agonists (effectors) and antagonists (anti-effectors) are equally trained and developed. It is therefore necessary to ensure that the flexor and extensor muscles of legs and arms are put under strain to the same degree, and that a muscular and functional imbalance does not arise. In practice, agonists and antagonists can be trained either in constant alternation or after each other.

The most important muscle group for duathletes is the extensor and flexor loop of the lower extremities. The flexor loop includes the front shin muscles, the rear upper thigh muscles (ischiocrural muscles) and the hip flexor muscles (iliopsoas). The extensor loop consists of the calf muscles, the front upper thigh muscles (quadriceps) and the large gluteal muscle.

Complex exercises covering several muscle groups, or alternatively isolated exercises, can be selected. As a matter of principle strength training should be carried out under supervision, for example in a sport studio. Below are a number of examples of exercises for maximum strength training. During all exercises make sure to breathe out during exertion.

Exercise 1: Leg Stretching in the Leg Press

The leg press should be adjusted so that the knee joint is bent at about 90 degrees in the starting position. While the leg is quickly stretched the foot is also stretched at the upper ankle. In the finishing position make sure that the knee is not completely stretched (risk of injuring the crucial ligaments). Then the burden is slowly and constantly returned to the starting position.

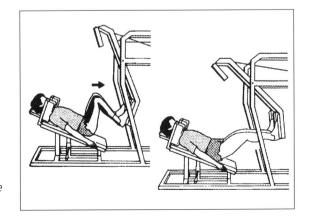

Fig. 43: Stretching the legs in the leg press

Exercise 2: Leg Bending on the Leg Curling Machine

The leg curling machine should be used in such a way that the axis of rotation of the knee joint is identical with that of the machine. While quickly bending the lower leg active locking of the hips should be ensured. In the slackening phase the burden is slowly and constantly returned to a slightly bent position of the knee.

Fig. 44: Leg bending on the leg curling machine

Exercise 3: Knee Stretching on the Strength Machine

In this isolated knee stretching exercise make sure that the pivot of the knee and of the machine match, and that the hollow of the knee is on the seat surface. When doing the fast stretching movements do not stretch the knee to the maximum possible.

In the slackening phase the leg is returned slowly and carefully to the starting position.

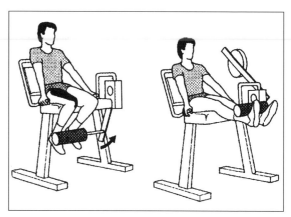

Fig. 45: Knee stretching on the strength machine

Exercise 4: Hip Stretching on the Strength Machine

On this strength machine, in the starting position with the knee raised high, there is resistance in the hollow of the knee. Using the ischiocrural muscles and the gluteal muscles the leg is quickly drawn to a rear stretching position. In doing so there is complete stretching in the hip.

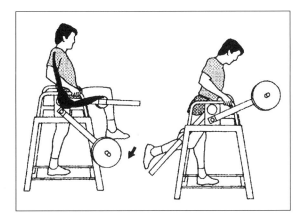

Fig. 46:
Hip stretching on the strength machine

11.5 Semi-Specific Strength Endurance Training

In semi-specific strength endurance training the same exercises are carried out as in maximum strength training, but with the following changes regarding intensity, amount and breaks: medium resistance (30-50%) is quickly overcome with a high number of repeats (20-30 repeats per series). The number of series increases from two or three in PP I to four or five in VP III. The duration of the breaks is 1-2 minutes.

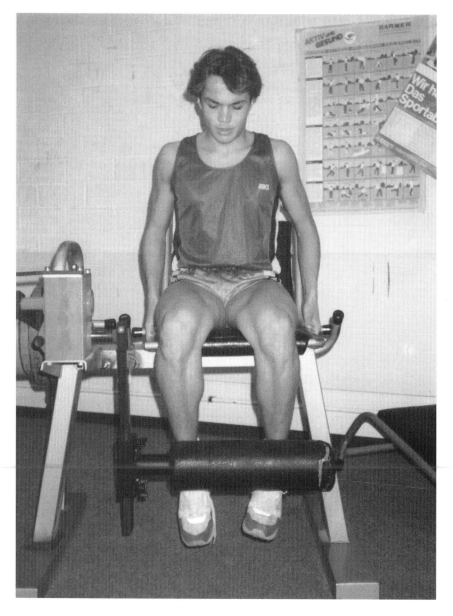

World champion Normann Stadler doing strength training as a youth

12 Women and Duathlon

– In Cooperation with Katja Kailer –

The sporting performance of women is often compared with that of men in sports medicine literature, whereby women usually come off worse: they run more slowly, they cannot jump as far or as high as men, they cannot lift such heavy weights and so on.

Performance differences based on gender have anatomical and physiological causes such as (cf. ENGELHARDT/KREMER 1986; PICKENHAIN et al. 1993):

* smaller anthropometric measurements (smaller body size),
* smaller dimensions of the oxygen intake, transporting and processing systems,
* larger fat stores and higher fat use,
* smaller proportion of muscle tissue,
* higher heart rate regulation,
* smaller proportion of haemoglobin (red corpuscles),
* smaller proportion of water in the body,
* lower protein usage,
* lower testosterone level (factor 20),
* less marked fitness capabilities (strength, speed),
* better coordination and more mobility,
* as well as, on the whole, about 10% lower absolute sporting performance than men in the same sports.

In these comparisons the man is taken as the starting point and the woman compared with him.

The reference for measurement of women's performance should not, however, be the male, but rather the female herself with the whole spectrum of her performance capacity. Sports medicine science, which in a positivist sense only describes differences found but does not consider social causes that can be responsible for current differences in performance, contributes to keeping the "myth of the stronger sex" alive.

It is also often not clear why the performance differences between men and women are emphasised so strongly, particularly when sports are involved in which the olympic comparatives "citius, altius, fortius" (latin = faster, higher, further) are decided in their favour by men in comparison to women.

It would be a mistake to deny or underestimate the biological nature of humans. When one considers, however, that for a long time women were denied the chance to make use of existing dispositions, experience and performance opportunities, and in some cases are still denied this today, then differences in performance capacity can also be interpreted socially. TIEDEMANN (1986, 80f.) cites as an example the strength "deficit" of women as opposed to men.

He says the medical-biological interpretation ignores social influences such as gender specific raising of children which is responsible to a great degree for the fact that the same biological aptitudes are either encouraged or hindered.

Also of interest is a paleoanthropological (study of life in earlier times) theory according to which in the stone age the sexes hardly differed with regard to the size and robustness of their bodies.

The gender specific characteristics of the total skeletal system, which today appear so clearly, did not develop naturally, so says this theory, but are rather a consequence of the division of labour between the sexes.

The above-mentioned differences seem unfavourable to women at first glance. For duathlon, however, and especially for the running discipline, they are often an advantage because they have a positive influence on endurance capability. In particular the favourable metabolism and the lower weight deserve mention.

Active body fat is a long-lasting reserve in the energy store. The enzyme system of women is well-equipped to reduce fats and convert them into energy. This compensates disadvantages in anaerobic capacity. With regard to aerobic endurance in the area of long-term endurance women produce comparable performances to men.

The differences between the sexes need not be pursued in depth in connection with sporting performance as it can be assumed that both men and women can practise duathlon – and of course they do – and the performance "borders" between the sexes (especially in amateur sport) are fluid.

From a training methodology point of view too there are basically no differences for women and men because of biological factors. For this reason the advice and suggestions in the various chapters of the book have the same relevance to both sexes and can be put into practice by both.

Emphasising gender specific differences can be important when health aspects are concerned that mainly affect one sex. The following pages therefore deal with topics specific to women which are certain to be of interest and importance to female endurance athletes.

This includes a digression on the subject of the disorder anorexia as it was found that many female endurance athletes have come down with this. The digression is especially intended to alert trainers and families so that they can recognise signs of the disorder and also to encourage athletes to analyse critically their own behaviour.

Iron Deficiency

A large number of women in endurance performance sport suffer from an iron deficiency. Some sports doctors used to think this was mainly connected with loss of blood in menstruation but these days the following factors are also considered responsible:

- poor dietary habits (not enough protein, too much fat, foods with low vitamin and iron content)
- oral intake of contraceptives (anti-baby pill)
- poor training structure (too intensive or training that builds-up too quickly).

What is also overlooked here is that when physical strain is high, so is iron consumption.

Female performance athletes should therefore regularly check their iron values and if necessary take supplements. Foodstuffs containing iron should play a large part in the daily menu (cf. chapter 14, p. 157ff.).

Menstruation

For many women their period is a hinderance for sport. From a sports medicine point of view, sport does not create any disadvantages, on the contrary, cramps and headaches are often eased by it. Even easy running is said to be particularly favourable to this effect. The way an individual feels during her period is of course very subjective, so every woman should decide for herself how much training she thinks she can handle at this time.

It used to be thought that the hormonal changes during menstruation could have negative effects on sporting performance. More recent research shows no correlation. The diverse overlying (external) factors should be seen as considerably more important than the influences caused by purely hormonal cyclical variations.

High performance female athletes' periods often come very irregularly or not at all over a long period (amenorrhoe). This is caused by great physical and psychological stress, too low a proportion of fat in the body and an increased level of testosterone. When training is reduced, menstruation usually begins again of its own accord. There are no effects on fertility: the rate of infertility amongst female endurance athletes is no greater than in the general population.

Pregnancy

During pregnancy endurance training needs not be stopped. It is advisable to train carefully in the first and last weeks of the pregnancy or to stop altogether at this time. It is also recommended to seek the advice of a doctor and discuss the degree of training strain with him or her.

Vitamins and Minerals

In addition to a healthy balanced diet, female endurance athletes should ensure they are getting plenty of calcium. Calcium and vitamin D deficiency are considered risk factors for the development of osteoporosis. Osteoporosis is characterised by a reduction in bone mass and a deterioration of the micro architecture which lead to increased bone brittleness and risk of fractures. In old age women are much more affected by this than men.

Despite the biologically equal abilities to do duathlon, in practice a clear dominance of men can be observed. The reasons for the low proportion of women are not clear and can only be guessed at: social factors, such as gender specific upbringing, could possibly play a major role.

Duathlon offers the chance to push through to one's physical limits and cross these limits; nature can be experienced very intensively here. Running and cycling are also sports which complement each other very well, which usually have a positive effect on the system and encourage the feeling for one's body. There should be an increase in the development of programmes oriented to the needs of women, such as separate starts for women in all events, to make duathlon more attractive to them.

Digression: Anorexia

"Anorexia nervosa" is suffered mainly by young women aged between ten and 25 years. It used to be assumed that young females were affected about a hundred times more than males. Today it is known that the number of young men who suffer eating disorders is also greatly increasing; it is assumed they make up 5-10% of all those affected (FARROW 1992).

People suffering from anorexia are observed to have a very distorted attitude to eating and fear of putting on weight, also a disturbed feeling for their bodies coupled with a clear denial of illness.

Bulimia (eat-vomit syndrome) is another form of eating disorder which is considered a chronic form of anorexia. In addition to refusing food, people suffering from bulimia frequently have massive attacks of high calorie gluttony, followed by measures such as excessive fasting, self-induced vomiting or abuse of laxatives and dehydrational medicaments.

Anorexia and bulimia are psychosomatic illnesses for which generally no single event can be identified as the cause. Concepts of ideal beauty and sexist values of western society play as much a role as massive problems in the relationships within families.

In addition to middle and long-distance running, sports with an above average number of anorexic female athletes are rhythmic sport gymnastics and competitive gymnastics – in other words, sports where too many pounds are a disadvantage. The number of anorexics among performance oriented female athletes is estimated by doctors and those affected to be about 25%. There are no figures available for duathlon.

Angelika Ross, a runner for twenty years and once affected, reports very poignantly on why female runners in particular are especially prone to anorexia: biomechanically it is an advantage to have a good strength-burden relationship.

In this respect reducing weight initially leads to a certain improvement in running ability. The motto "the lighter, the faster" takes over. Because for many female athletes running becomes their meaning in life, everything else loses significance and they often overlook the fact that life outside of running becomes more and more strenuous as a result of this obsession. Also, daily training makes them used to conquering their "weaker self", so it is not surprising that they are "especially susceptible to an addiction that does not promise quick pleasure but rather to a certain extent demands hard work" (ROSS 1994, 63)

As aneroxia increases, the faculty of self-assessment gets worse and worse, which means that women still consider themselves too fat when they are only "skin and bones".

If the extreme reduction in nutrition creates a nutrient deficit and electrolyte disorders, this often leads to a fall in performance. The anorexic will, however, often deny the cause.

Trainers and families in particular should be very careful about criticising female athletes about their weight.

Rather they should be aware of more or less serious eating disorders, which can be indicated by the following factors independent of actual weight:

- great fear of putting on weight,
- being slim is seen as a guarantee for the solution of all other problems,
- constantly checking weight, even minor variations are seen as major catastrophes,
- dieting as a permanent habit, trying out more and more different types of diet,
- self-induced vomiting after supposedly taking in too many calories,
- regular taking of laxatives, dehydration medicaments, appetite suppressors,
- always thinking about eating, bad conscience every time food is consumed,
- attacks of ravenous appetite because of under-nourishment, followed by guilt, depressions, self-hatred, thoughts of suicide,
- excessive sporting activity in order to get the body's (food) needs "under control", as self-inflicted punishment for what is felt to be too high food consumption, or "saving" calories before a large meal,
- reduced fluid consumption to avoid "concentration of water" in the body, or excessive consumption of low calorie or no calorie drinks to combat the feeling of "emptiness" in the stomach,
- period does not come because of physical overexertion coupled with energy intake that is too low (cf. MEERMANN/VANDEREYCKEN 1987).

The consequences of eating disorders are diverse: major health problems can arise due to lack of nourishment, damage in the stomach and intestine area and in the gullet, tooth decay, hair loss, disruption of the electrolyte store and, as already mentioned, problems with menstruation.

People use anorexia to try and cover up deep seated doubts. Often they have been given the feeling of not being good enough, or different from others. They therefore usually also have trouble with relationships or even suffer social isolation.

The aim should therefore always be psychotherapy, because "just" talking is usually not enough to cause a change. Putting pressure on the person is pointless because it will only be countered. Patience and understanding are most important, fast cures should not be expected.

An illness which takes a person to their existential limits will not suddenly disappear as long as the factors behind it have not been resolved.

13 Training and Race Analysis

13.1 Training Analysis

In order to best develop one's own abilities, achieve the desired training effects, and finally the corresponding race performance, complete documentation of all relevant training data is absolutely necessary. The complex presentation of the various aspects of training allows an in-depth analysis on the basis of which possible training errors can be tracked down and a revised training schedule can be adopted.

This can of course be done especially effectively with the help of a computer, but handwritten notes also offer good opportunities to monitor progress as long as the recording has been done sensibly and clearly. On the next page you will find a form for setting up a training and race journal that fullfils the requirements of a modern endurance training monitoring system.

13.2 Race Analysis

The race analysis is an important building block for judging performance capacity. This assumes that the race was objectively evaluated and conscientiously recorded. Over the page is a form for race analysis in which the main relevant data can be entered.

In practice there are many possibilities for race analysis. Firstly you can compare your own performance to that of other race participants. This is called a cross-sectional analysis. Secondly you can compare your performance with your own performance in earlier races. And thirdly you can analyse your race performance in relationship to the performance that could have been expected from the actual training done. The latter two are referred to as longitudinal section comparisons.

Cross-Sectional Comparison

Placing and race time can be used for a cross-sectional comparison. The placing gives a first glance at the performance delivered. A top placing in a duathlon race gives you a good feeling – it strengthens the athlete's self-confidence and motivates for further training.

	Time	Running				Cycling				Other gymn. strength	Comments
		RECOM	BE 1	BE 2	RSE	RECOM	BE 1	BE 2	RSE		
		km min	km min	km min	km min	km min	km min	km min	km min	min	
MO											Pulse at rest
TU											Pulse at rest
WE											Pulse at rest
TH											Pulse at rest
FR											Pulse at rest
SA											Pulse at rest
SU											Pulse at rest
&											

Weekly record: Duathlon   Week: _____ from _____ to _____ 19 ___
Name: _____   Club: _____
Address: _____   DOB: _____

Training region (targets)

	Running		Cycling	
	HR (1/min)	V (min/km)	HR (1/min)	V (min/km)
RECOM				
BE 1				
BE 2				
RSE				

Total amount

km		h:min
Cycling		
Running		
Other		
Total		

Fig. 47: Form for photocopying: weekly record

Race Analysis

Name: _____   Club: _____
(Age) Category: _____   Season: _____

Event	Date	Distance	Time	Placing	Comments
					Pulse at Rest
					Pulse at Rest
					Pulse at Rest
					Pulse at Rest
					Pulse at Rest
					Pulse at Rest
					Pulse at Rest
					Pulse at Rest
					Pulse at Rest

Fig. 48: Form for race analysis

It is also obvious, however, that a placing is very much dependent on the performance level of the race as a whole. A top placing in a novice duathlon or at a German Cup event must be evaluated completely differently.

The analysis is more reliable when the race time is taken into consideration. Then the time difference to the overall winner or the age category winner can be studied. This procedure is more accurate if you also take the split times for running and cycling into account. Because the route profile and route length of various duathlon races are usually not comparable it is recommended to work out the differences as a percentage.

Heart Rate Analysis and Longitudinal Comparison

For most athletes the exact analysis of their own performance is in the foreground. It begins a few seconds after the race already with generally emotional statements like "Today I felt really good"; "I had absolutely no pressure on the bike"; "I'm satisfied with my performance"; "I didn't get my pulse up at all"; "I was too fast on the first run"; "After the cycling I had muscle problems running" etc. Not until a certain time afterwards (the next day) is an objective evaluation possible. It is helpful for the following analysis if the heart rate during the race was stored by an HR measuring device. The course of the heart rate values reflects the physical strain on the body very closely.

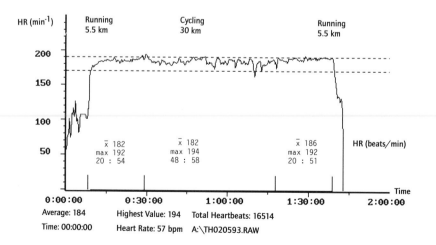

Fig. 49: *Heart rate progression in duathlon (5.5 - 30 - 5.5 km) of an 18 year old athlete*

Example 1:

The heart rate progression of an 18 year old duathlete was analysed. The two 5.5 km runs were on a flat course. The athlete took almost exactly the same time for both runs. In the heart rate behaviour there are only minimal differences. The average heart rate in the second run is 4 beats/min higher, the maximum heart rate is the same in both runs at 192 beats/min. From the HR curve an increase can be recognised before the change to cycling, indicating a brief increase in running speed (short burst of speed). Over the average profile cycling course with longer climbs of up to 7% a maximum heart rate of 194 beats/min is reached. On average the cycling heart rates are in the region of the running heart rates. There is no falling or rising trend in the heart rate progression shown in the HR record.

Interpretation:

The athlete has divided up the race as a whole well. The first and second run were done at relatively constant, submaximal intensity of effort. In the cycling too the athlete remained in this intensity region. There are no signs of exhaustion. Not recommended is the increase in intensity of effort just before the change to the next discipline. Muscles that are overacidic can considerably impair cycling performance over the first few kilometres.

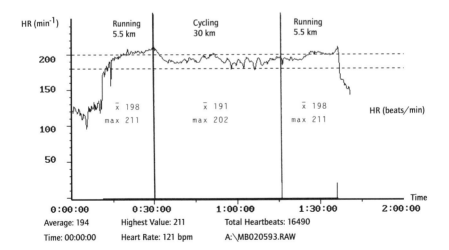

Fig. 50: Heart rate progression in duathlon (5.5 - 30 - 5.5 km) of a 19 year old athlete

Example 2:
This athlete structured his race over the same course completely differently. The progression of the heart rate curve shows that the exertion heart rate in the first run constantly increased up to a maximum of 211 beats/min. After the change to cycling the HR fell back to 184 beats/min. The average cycling HR was 191 beats/min. The running heart rates were on average 14 beats higher than the cycling heart rates. In the final dash for overall 3rd placing there was another rise in the heart rate to a maximum value of 211 beats/min.

Interpretation:
The high heart-circulation effort at the beginning and end of the race indicates a good performance situation. The athlete demonstrates strength of will and high muscular mobilisation capacity. Both can only be achieved if the body is sufficiently regenerated. From a performance physiology point of view the athlete did not optimally structure his race. Because of the 100% exertion in the first run, and the resultingly large build-up of lactate ("overacidity of the muscles"), the athlete could not initially make the most of his abilities in the cycling.

Only once lactate has been reduced can the intensity of effort be increased, as is recognisable by the increase in the heart rate. After the second change too the athlete had to run the first 1.5 km at lower intensity. The cause of this can also be too much intensity in the last cycling kilometres. Possibly no specific coupled training was carried out so that the athlete had functional adjustment difficulties to cope with.

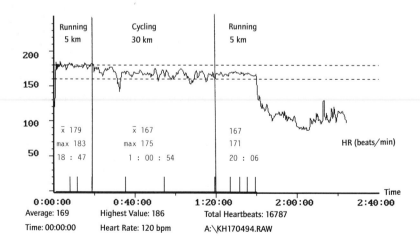

Fig. 51: Heart rate progression in duathlon (5 - 30 - 5 km) of a 35 year old athlete

Example 3:

This heart rate record comes from a 35 year old athlete who took part in the Söhre duathlon. This race was carried out on very hilly terrain which, however, was not expressed in the temporal progression of the heart rate curve. The heart rate values changed extremely little on the hill running course, i.e. the organic effort remained roughly the same running up and down hill. This required a high variability in running speed, high running coordinational ability and a good running style.

The entire race was run with at an average heart rate of 169 beats/min. The highest heart rates were reached in the first run. The average value was 179 beats/min. In the cycling and the second run the average value was 12 beats/min lower.

Interpretation:

The lower HR values in the second run indicate that the athlete possibly overtaxed himself in the first run, had too little aerobic capacity and/or falsely evaluated his performance capability.

More and more athletes orient themselves towards their heart rate in races.

14 Dietary Recommendations

– In Cooperation with Kirsten Brüning* –

It is not easy to give up habits, and there is no question that this also applies to eating habits. The dietary recommendations made in this chapter can, however, help any athlete to stabilise their state of health, make the most of their potential and optimise their performance. The athletes themselves decide whether they want to avoid dietary mistakes and stick to dietary recommendations that aid performance. Nutrition is one of the factors they can easily influence themselves to gain benefits for their performance ability (cf. Fig. 1, p. 10)

Research shows that athletes in general consume too few carbohydrates, vitamins and minerals with their food, but instead eat too much fat. This diet is particularly unfavourable for endurance athletes because it has been proven that the provision of nourishment to the muscles and their ability to take strain in the endurance region can be optimised with a carbohydrate rich, low fat diet. To cover energy needs the following percentage proportion of nutrients is considered especially beneficial to the performance ability of endurance athletes: 60-65% carbohydrates, 20-25% fats and 10.15% proteins (Fig. 52).

The athlete's particular task is to adjust his diet to the requirements of training and of races, especially when he wants to achieve super compensation effects (see Fig. 55, p. 178). To make it easier to change to a healthy, balanced diet that improves performance we will now explain the foundations of nutrition for endurance athletes.

---

*Dipl. Oecotrophologist, nutritional consultant to various sports associations, member of the work group "Sports and Nutrition" at German Olympic bases.

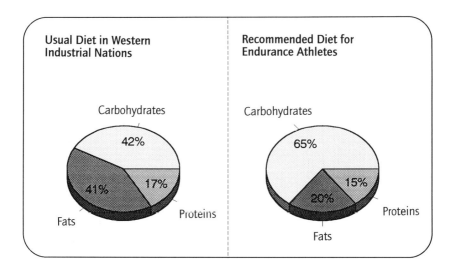

Fig. 52: Percentage proportion of main nutrients in daily energy intake

14.1 Staple Diet

To optimise performance capacity we need a number of essential nutrients which the body cannot, or at least not sufficiently, produce itself.

These include vitamins, minerals, some amino acids and polyunsaturated fatty acids. These nutrients can be taken into the body with the aid of a balanced staple diet.

The duathlete needs food with a high nutrient density, i.e. which contains a relatively high percentage of essential nutrients per energy unit laid down.

Three basic rules apply to the diet of endurance athletes: it should emphasise *carbohydrates, be low in fat and protein enriched.*

The food pyramid (Fig. 53) illustrates a staple diet: The wide base of the pyramid indicates the great significance of fluid and carbohydrate consumption which should make up the main part of our daily diet. The higher up the pyramid, the smaller the amounts of the foodstuffs shown should be. At the top of the pyramid are semi-luxury foods which we should – if at all – rarely eat and only in small amounts. The endurance athlete's staple diet thus consists of:

Food Pyramid

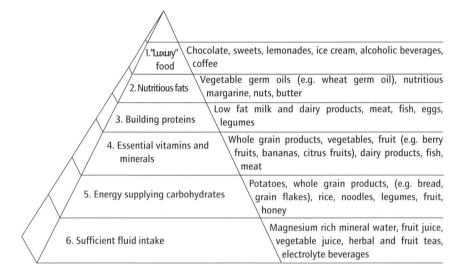

1."Luxury" food	Chocolate, sweets, lemonades, ice cream, alcoholic beverages, coffee
2. Nutritious fats	Vegetable germ oils (e.g. wheat germ oil), nutritious margarine, nuts, butter
3. Building proteins	Low fat milk and dairy products, meat, fish, eggs, legumes
4. Essential vitamins and minerals	Whole grain products, vegetables, fruit (e.g. berry fruits, bananas, citrus fruits), dairy products, fish, meat
5. Energy supplying carbohydrates	Potatoes, whole grain products, (e.g. bread, grain flakes), rice, noodles, legumes, fruit, honey
6. Sufficient fluid intake	Magnesium rich mineral water, fruit juice, vegetable juice, herbal and fruit teas, electrolyte beverages

Figg. 53: Food Pyramid

1. Sufficient Consumption of Fluids

Before, during and after sporting exertion you must ensure a sufficient supply of fluids because through the increased production of sweat the body loses water and important minerals.

A fluid deficiency leads to dehydration and thus reduced performance capacity. Endurance athletes should therefore never skip the drinking stop in a race. The body does not react until a fluid loss reducing performance has already taken place, so duathletes should drink regularly, *before* they start to feel thirsty.

Sources:
Suitable drinks for athletes are mineral water with a high magnesium content (more than 100 mg magnesium/litre), fruit juice and mineral water mixtures (proportion of

Fluid deficiency leads to reduced performance capacity.

juice to mineral water: 1:2 to 1:3), vegetable juices, freshly pressed fruit juices, slightly sweetened fruit tea, electrolyte drinks (hypotonic to isotonic, low in mineral salts and carbohydrates).

During endurance exertion small amounts of carbohydrates in drinks (5% sugar solution – about 50 g sugar per litre of water) contribute to the stabilisation of the blood sugar level and improve the absorption of minerals in the intestines. The ingestion of sodium and carbohydrates (glucose, saccharose or maltodextrine) assists the absorption of fluids in the intestines.

Quantity:
On days of no sporting activity it is recommended to drink at least 1.5 litres of fluids spread throughout the day to meet the body's water requirements. On training days an additional water requirement of 1.0 to 1.5 litres per hour of physical activity is advised in moderate climates. A criterion for meeting the needs of fluids is the urine colour: it should be as light as possible.

2. Energy Supplying Carbohydrates (= Starch and Sugar)

A diet rich in carbohydrates raises the amount of glycogen in the muscles and thus their resilience during endurance activities. Glycogen is the storage form of carbohydrates in the body. The better the energy reserves are filled, the higher the athlete's performance capacity. If the carbohydrate reserves are used up too early it can result in hypoglycaemia (too little sugar in the blood), accompanied by such symptoms as dizziness or signs of weakness.

Carbohydrate holders with roughage should be given preference because roughage (plant components which humans cannot digest) has a braking effect on the blood sugar curve when one eats carbohydrate rich food. This mechanism ensures that the muscle, nerve and brain cells receive a constant supply of glucose that is tailored to their needs.

Sources:
The recommended complex carbohydrates or polysaccharides (starch, dextrine) are contained in wholemeal bread, muesli, bananas, potatoes, vegetables and noodles. Monosaccharides (glucose) or duosaccharides (saccharose = sugar), as found in sweets, lemonades, honey and jams, are processed too quickly by the body and are suitable for brief exertion (e.g. sprints). They contribute little to blood sugar stabilisation.

Quantity:

The carbohydrate intake of a diet conscious duathlete should be about 55% of daily energy supply.

3. A Balanced Protein Supply

In highly intensive training phases (e.g. in a training camp) endurance athletes have an increased need for proteins because demands on them often extend to the limits of their resilience. In this case the proteins are drawn on as a reserve to meet energy requirements because the main energy suppliers (carbohydrates and fats) are no longer available in sufficient quantities. Proteins should not, however, be drawn on over a longer period of time as a source of energy, or else a situation of overtraining will arise. High protein consumption can lead to wear and tear on cell membranes, cell damage and to reduction of muscle.

A reduction in protein can be established medically through higher serum urea values in the morning. If a urea value of over 8 mmol/l is measured in blood from the ear capillaries the amount of training strain must be reduced immediately (cf. Fig. 60, p. 190).

Sources:

Good sources of protein are grain products, legumes, milk, dairy products, fish, meat and eggs. The combining of vegetable and animal protein increases the biological valency of the food protein so that it can be better used for building up of the body's own protein (e.g. muscle build-up). A balance is achieved if 60% of the protein supply is from vegetable and 40% from animal protein sources.

Quantity:

A duathlete's staple protein requirement is 10 to 15% of daily energy intake.

4. Few, but High Quality Fats

Fat also serves to provide energy but it consumes about 13% more oxygen than the combustion of carbohydrates and is only increasingly used to gain energy during longer lasting endurance efforts at low to medium intensity.

The body cannot produce *polyunsaturated fatty acids* itself. They are an important component of the cell membrane and influence cell metabolism among other things. A further important component of vegetable oils is vitamin E, a natural antioxidant that protects the unsaturated fatty acids in the body from oxidation. The fat supply should consist of at least *1/3 polyunsaturated fatty acids, 1/3 monounsaturated fatty acids* and *a maximum 1/3 saturated fatty acids.*

Sources:
The recommended polyunsaturated fatty acids can be found in vegetable oils such as sunflower seed, or wheat germ oil and in nuts. Suitable fats for an athlete's diet are also vegetable spreads such as diet margarine with a minimum of 50% unsaturated fatty acids.

Quantity:
Daily fat intake should make up a maximum of 30% of energy sources. The advised value for daily cholesterol intake is a maximum 300 mg which corresponds to the recommendations of the German Nutrition Society (Deutsche Gesellschaft für Ernährung, DGE 1992, 30) for nutrient consumption.

5. Vitamins and Minerals Essential for Life

These too are essential nutrients the human body needs to live because it either does not produce them itself or not in sufficient quantities, and therefore has to get them from food. Of special significance to duathletes are the vitamins of the B complex (indispensable for the conversion of energy) and Vitamin C (strengthens the immune system) as well as the antioxidants vitamin E, C and beta carotene (a form of vitamin A). The performance oriented athlete also needs sufficient quantities of the minerals magnesium and potassium (for the muscle functions and glycogen storage), iron (oxygen transport), zinc (building up protein) and iodine (for optimal functioning of the thyroid glands).

Because of the close relationship between energy and nutrient supply, athletes who wish to keep their weight down (e.g. female long-distance runners) are more at risk of a vitamin and mineral deficiency. A nutrient rich staple diet can, however, prevent such deficiencies.

Sources:
Vitamins and minerals are in fruit, vegetables, wholemeal products, potatoes, milk, dairy products, fish and meat. The functions of the various vitamins and minerals, as well as good nutrient sources, are shown on pages 164 and 165.

Quantity:
Vitamins and minerals should be consumed with food daily if possible, at the least the weekly balance should be maintained.

Table 14a: Functions of minerals and good sources

	MINERAL	FUNCTION/EFFECTS	MINERAL RICH FOODS
Trace Elements	Sodium	• binds water in tissue • determines osmotic pressure • activates enzymes	Common salt, salty foods (e.g. cheese, sausage)
	Chloride	• binds water in tissue • component of gastric acid	Common salt, salty foods (e.g.cheese, sausage)
	Potassium	• draws water from tissue (counterpart of sodium) • involved in building up glycogen	Bananas, potatoes, dried fruit, spinach, mushrooms
	Calcium	• component of bones and teeth • sensitivity of muscles • stabilises cell membranes • involved in transmission of stimuli in the nervous system	Milk, dairy products, leeks, mangold, green cabbage, broccoli,French beans, sardines
	Magnesium	• component of bones and teeth • activates energy metabolism enzymes • involved in neuro-muscular transmission of stimuli and muscle contraction	legumes, whole grain products, milk, dairy products, meat, liver, poultry, potatoes, cauliflower, raspberries, soya beans, bananas
	Phosphor	• phosphates are ingredients for bones and teeth • important for energy storage	practically all foodstuffs
Mineral Elements	Iron	• involved in oxygen transport • component of enzymes • important for the immune system	Meat, small goods, wheat germ, wholemeal products, corn salad
	Iodine	• Component of the thyroid gland hormones	Ocean fish, eggs, milk*
	Fluoride	• responsible for the hardening of the tooth enamel	Mineral water, grain products, eggs*
	Zinc	• functions as enzyme co-factor • important for insulin storage • strengthens the immune system	offal, muscle meat, dairy products, eggs, pike, duck,crustaceans/shellfish
	Selenium	• protects against free roots	Muscle meat, grain products (barley), legumes*

* Mineral content of the foodstuffs is dependent on the varying content of the soils.

Table 14b: Functions of vitamins and good sources

	VITAMIN	FUNCTION/EFFECTS	VITAMIN RICH FOODS
Fat soluble	A (Retinol)	• involved in sight process • protective function for skin and mucous membranes	Carrots, green cabbage, spinach, milk, margarine, butter
	D (Calciferol)	• bone mineralisation • regulation of calcium and phosphor metabolism	Herring, mackerel, eel, salmon, liver, egg yolk
	E (Tocopherol)	• protects unsaturated fatty acids and vitamin A from free roots	Wheat germ or sunflower seed oil, margarine, nuts
	K (Phyllochinon Menachinon)	• component of blood coagulating factors	Green salads (e.g. lettuce), cauliflower, cress, tomatoes, milk, liver
Water soluble	B1 (Thiamin)	• important for the nervous system and energy metabolism	Wholemeal bread, oat flakes, pork, potatoes, legumes
	B2 (Riboflavin)	• involved in carbohydrate, fat and protein metabolism	Milk, dairy products, fish, meat, eggs, wholemeal bread
	Niacin (Nicotine acid)	• component of enzymes involved in energy metabolism	Peanuts, peas, meat, salmon, wheat bran, wholemeal bread
	B6 (Pyrodoxin)	• regulates protein metabolism • has a function in the nervous system	Poultry, pork, fish, cabbage varieties, French beans, lentils, corn salad
	Folic acid	• responsible for the maturing of red and white corpuscles • important for cell division and building of new cells	Soya sprouts, wholemeal products, tomatoes, cucumber, wheatgerm, cabbage varieties, potatoes
	Pantothenic acid	• significant for break down processes of carbohydrates, fats and amino acids	Broccoli, cauliflower, meat, milk, wholemeal bread, water melons
	Biotin	• involved in building up carbohydrates and fatty acids	Soya beans, egg yolk, nuts, oat flakes, sardines, lentils, cauliflower
	B12 (Cobalamin)	• activates the vitamin folic acid • important for blood formation	Herring, sea fish like cod, beef, eggs, curd
	C (Ascorbic acid)	• strengthens the immune system • improves iron intake from food • involved in formation and functional maintenance of connective tissue	Citrus fruits, tomatoes, green peppers, potatoes, black currants

Type of Energy Provision in Relationship to Duration of Effort

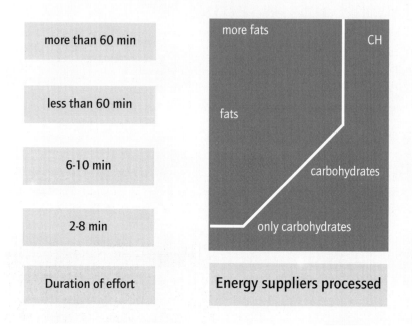

Fig. 54: Nutrient proportion of energy provision in relationship to duration of effort (modified from GEISS/HAMM 1992)

14.2 "Luxury" Foods and Beverages

These foods include coffee, tea, alcoholic beverages, soft drinks, ice cream, chocolate and other sweets. They are "empty calorie transporters" because they only contain small amounts of vitamins and minerals. Endurance athletes often reach for sweets because the lowered blood sugar level during and after training strain can lead to desire for sweet foods.

This should, however, be satisfied with fruit or dried fruit, ensuring that the athlete does not take in too much additional energy and at the same time is provided with the essential nutrients. Coffee and tea can be drunk in reasonable amounts (2-3 cups per day). These drinks have a diuretic effect, however, and take from the athlete the important transporter and solvent water as well as minerals contained in it.

Alcohol

Athletes should avoid alcoholic beverages as the primary thirst quencher after training or a race because alcohol can have both immediate and lasting effects on the body system. For example, it delays the build-up of energy reserves in the recovery phase after physical exertion and thus interferes with the development of performance.

In sport alcohol is the most frequently abused luxury consumable; at many sporting events alcoholic beverages are offered for sale.

The financial support of main events by breweries also contributes to legitimising the connection between sport and alcohol. This can have an effect on young athletes who can come to believe a "booze-up" is part of the victory celebration after a race.

A much too frequent scene: the athlete indulges in a beer straight after a race.

Sometimes one comes across the opinion that after hard training the fluid loss can be made good with a few beers. The assumption that beer contains important carbohydrates is also used to excuse excessive alcohol consumption. In reality the proportion of carbohydrates in beer in comparison to fruit juices is very small. For example 0.3 l of light beer only has 6 g of regular carbohydrates (which are different to the empty calories in alcohol) compared with about 50 g in the same amount of fruit juice.

On top of that, alcohol is an ergolytic drug. It is an organic solvent that can be easily and completely absorbed by the stomach. During this process the stomach and mucous membranes can become irritated. This reduces the intake of nutrients, especially of vitamins and minerals. Increased alcohol consumption can also not only lead to tissue damage but to a greater proportion of body fat as well.

The American College of Sports Medicine has come to the following four conclusions with regard to alcohol:

1. It interferes with psychomotor abilities.
2. It changes physiological functions in a way that does not favour improvement in physical performance.
3. It reduces the performance ability of the muscles.
4. It can interfere with temperature regulation of the body.

All of these factors support the thesis that regular alcohol consumption is not compatible with recommendations for a performance oriented diet suitable for carrying out sports.

14.3   Nutrition in the Course of the Day

Not only the right choice of foods and beverages is important for a healthy diet but also the spacing of the meals throughout the day. Nutritional consultants recommend spreading daily nutritional energy over five to six smaller meals. In contrast to the usual three large meals this meal structure has the advantage that the digestive organs are put under less strain and the nutrients can be better extracted from the food. This has a positive effect on a duathlete's performance capacity especially in the competition period.

In the preparatory periods endurance athletes have achieved positive results through reduced food consumption during the day (fat metabolism training) and a larger, carbohydrate rich meal, in the evening. It is difficult, but important, to adapt all meals to training and race times.

If you train or race in the morning you must eat enough at breakfast. When sports events are on in the late afternoon or evening the carbohydrate rich snack must not be forgotten.

14.4   Nutrition in the Course of the Year

The actual proportion of energy supplying main nutrients (carbohydrates, fats, proteins) in a diet suitable for a particular sport is dependent on the duration and intensity of training. In practice it is also necessary to take the varying demands over the course of the year into consideration.

To achieve effective energy provision, and to replenish glycogen stores as fast as possible after training, endurance athletes should have a very carbohydrate rich diet. Table 15 shows how to select the proportions of main nutrients in the daily diet in the various sports periods.

Table 15: Proportion of main nutrients in the daily diet in individual sports periods

Period (duration)	Main nutrients (in %)		
	Carbohydrates	Fats	Proteins
Preparatory period (2-6 months)	55-60	25-30	10-15
Competition period (about 2 months)	60-65	20-25	10-15
Race week (2 – 6 days)			
• protein rich (3 days)	30-35	25-30	30-35
• carbohydrate rich (3 days)	65-70	15-20	10-15
• during the race	65-70	15-20	10-15

14.4.1   Preparatory Period

Training in the preparatory period is characterised by long lasting effort at a relatively low level of stimulus. During constant endurance work over an hour, energy needs are covered in almost equal parts by oxidation from carbohydrates and fats.

This does not at all mean that duathletes must have a diet that is equally rich in carbohydrates and fats, for carbohydrates are the most important energy source for duathletes. Its percentage of total energy intake should be at least 55%. Fat rich animal foods that mainly have fatty acids with long carbon chains are hard to digest, and place a strain on metabolism (e.g. through increased cholestorol intake). They have the effect of reducing performance when the fatty acids are increasingly deposited in depot fat as a mass that does not metabolise well.

Because as a rule the subcutaneous fat tissue offers sufficient fat for gaining energy, a daily fat intake of 25-30% of total food energy is recommended.

For sufficient provision of the body with protein, the protein intake should not fall below a value of 1.5 g/kg body weight/day. This corresponds to an energy proportion of between 10-15% (GEISS/HAMM 1992, 190). This amount of protein helps the endurance athlete to maintain muscle mass and build up enzymes and hormones which regulate the diverse metabolic processes for optimal performance capacity.

What should duathletes eat on a training day in the preparatory period?

Here are two examples of dietary plans:

1st Example:

Female duathlete, age: 23 years, height: 173 cm, weight: 60 kg, training in the BE 1 region, 4 hours cycling (about 25 km/h), energy requirement: about 2,800 kcal (= 11.7 MJ) per day.

Proportion of main nutrients of food energy:

55-60% carbohydrates	=	385-420 g
25-30% fat	=	70-93 g
10-15% protein	=	70-105 g

Daily Recommendation When Training in BE 1 in Preparatory Period I

4-5 slices of wholemeal bread (200 g)	*or*	3-4 slices of wholemeal bread (120 g) and 50 g grain flakes (2 – 3 dsp)
300 g potatoes (3 – 4 medium sized)	*or*	120 g wholemeal noodles (cooked)
350 g vegetables (cooked) and 200 g vegetable juice	*or*	150 g vegetables (raw or cooked) and 400 g vegetable juice
300 g fresh fruit and 200 g fruit juice	*or*	250 g fresh fruit 200 g fruit juice 30 g dried fruits
350 g milk (1.5% fat) and 100 g curd cheese (20% fat)	*or*	250 g sour dairy products (1.5%) and 2 slices of cheese (30% F.i.dr.m.) (60 g)
150 g lean meat, poultry or fish	*or*	80 g soya products (e.g. tofu) and 1 egg
20 g margarine (3 tsp) and 15 g olive oil (1 dsp)	*or*	25 g butter (3-4 tsp) and 10 g sunflower seed oil (1-2 tsp)
30 g honey or jam (2 dsp)	*or*	10 g sugar (2 tsp) and 20 g honey or jam
30 g nuts (2 dsp) and 2-3 wholemeal biscuits (30 g)	*or*	3-4 wholemeal biscuits (40 g) and 1 bar of chocolate (20 g)
3 l mineral water and 1 l fruit tea	*or*	2 l fruit juice+mineral water (mixture juice to water 1:3), 1 l fruit tea, 1 l mineral water

2nd Example:

Male duathlete, age: 27 years, height: 180 cm, weight: 70 kg, training in the BE 2 region, e.g. 8 x 1,000 m runs, about16 km/h, training duration about one hour, energy requirement: about 3,000 kcal (= 12.5 MJ) per day.

Proportion of main nutrients of food energy:

55-60% carbohydrates	=	412-450 g
25-30% fat	=	83-100 g
10-15% protein	=	75-113 g

Daily Recommendation When Training in BE 2 in Preparatory Period II

4 slices of wholemeal bread (160 g) and 2 rye bread rolls (80 g)	*or*	3 slices of wholemeal bread (120 g) and 60 g grain flakes (2 – 3 dsp)
150 g natural rice (cooked)	*or*	350 g potatoes (4 – 5 medium size)
200 g vegetables (steamed) 150 salad vegetables	*or*	150 g legumes (cooked) and 200 g vegetables (steamed)
200 g fresh fruit and 60 g fruit pieces	*or*	250 g fruit juice and 150 g fresh fruit
250 g milk (1.5% fat) 50 g curd cheese (20% fat) and 150 g yoghurt (1.5% fat)	*or*	150 g sour milk 2 slices of cheese (30% F.i.dr.m.) (60 g) and 20 g cream cheese (1 dsp)
150 g lean meat, poultry or fish and 1 slice of lean sliced sausage	*or*	50 g soya products (e.g. tofu) 1 egg and 1 slice of ham (30 g)

Women running leaders at Zofingen

World champion Normann Stadler

German champion and European vice-champion Ralf Eggert

Cross country skiing: efficient cross training for duathletes

20 g butter (3 tsp) and 15 g wheatgerm (1 dsp)	*or*	25 g spreading fat (3 – 4 dsp) and 10 g sunflower seed oil (1- 2 tsp)
30 g honey or jam (2 dsp)	*or*	10 g sugar (2 tsp) and 20 g honey or jam
120 g fruit cake and 15 g nuts (1 dsp)	*or*	4 – 5 wholemeal biscuits (50 g) and 1 bar of chocolate (20 g)
2 l mineral water and 1 l fruit tea	*or*	1 l fuit juice+mineral water (mixture juice to water 1:3) 1 l fruit tea, 1 l mineral water

Abbreviations: dsp= desertspoon; tsp=teaspoon; F.i.dr.m.=fat in dry mass; l=litre

14.4.2   Competition Period

In the competition period the carbohydrate proportion of the diet is increased while fats are reduced. In order to create a maximum super compensation effect in the race week a special dietary and training plan is followed about 8-10 days before a major race.

Super Compensation

It is possible to increase the glycogen stores of the working muscles using a combination of intensive training and a carbohydrate rich diet. In doing so the race week is divided into three phases: the protein rich phase, the carbohydrate rich phase and the phase during the race.

In order to make use of the effect of super compensation exactly on race day all training and dietary measures must be exactly coordinated with each other. At the beginning there is a large amount of aerobic or intensive aerobic-anaerobic training two days before the actual start of the dietary adjustment with the objective of emptying the glycogen stores as much as possible. This is followed by the protein rich phase (s. Fig. 55).

In the **protein rich phase** (lasts about three days), first the proportion of protein is increased to 30-35% and that of fats to 25-30% of daily energy supply. The carbohydrate proportion has a maximum percentage of 35%. Training is carried on at medium duration and intensity of effort.

This leads to an almost complete emptying of the glycogen stores in the muscles and the liver. The protein rich diet ends on the third day after highly intensive training.

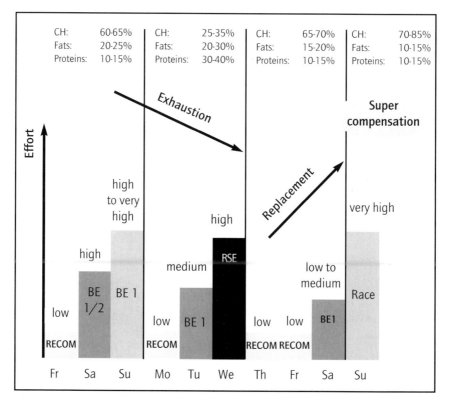

Fig. 55: Super compensation – training and dietary preparation for a duathlon race

Then follows a **carbohydrate rich phase** (duration about three days) which is characterised by a relative carbohydrate proportion of 65-70% of daily energy intake. Training is in the regenerative region. In this way the emptied glycogen stores are filled up again to a maximum.

Owing to the training stimuli the body is not used to, and the dietary adjustment, the glycogen stores of the muscles and liver of untrained people can be increased by up to 50% (GEISS/HAMM 1992, (91), and of trained athletes by up to 10-20% above the normal glycogen content.

In the third phase, in the time **during the race**, the best prepared energy stores are used to get a corresponding performance. Table 16 shows concrete dietary guidelines and food recommendations for the week of the race.

Because of the extreme pressure on metabolism the principle of super compensation explained here should only be practised before three main races per year at the most in order to spare the body. Experience has shown that applying the diets can lead to reductions in physical and mental well-being. Symptoms of this are weariness or dizzinesss, nausea and lack of motivation, which negatively influence an athlete's resilience. This is the result of the hunger metabolism on protein-fat rich days which is caused by the lack of carbohydrates.

Table 16: Dietary recommendation for the week of the race using the super compensation principle

Days	Dietary Form	Recommended Foodstuffs
1 2	Staples (carbo-hydrate rich, protein optimised, fat reduced)	**Main energy sources**: Whole grain products, pasta, potatoes, rice, vegetables, legumes, fruit; **Supplemented with:** low fat dairy products, lean meat, fish, poultry; eggs, little spreading and cooking fat, few luxury goods and sweets, sweet pastries; **Drinks:** daily at least 2 litres of low calorie fluids (magnesium rich mineral water, diluted fruit juices, herbal and fruit teas, electrolyte drinks);

3	Protein-fat rich diet	**Main energy sources:** low fat milk and dairy products, lean meat, fish, poultry, legumes, whole grain products, potatoes;
4		**Supplemented with:** pasta, rice, vegetables, fruit, little cakes and sweets, little spreading and cooking fat;
		Drinks: see days 1 and 2 (at least 3 l daily)
6	Carbohydrate rich	**Main energy sources:** 6th day: diet whole meal products, potatoes, vegetables, from the 7th day on also more rice, pasta, fruit, sweet pastries;
7		**Supplemented with:** little low fat milk and dairy products, – lean meat, poultry, fish, eggs, legumes, very little spreading and cooking fats; few luxury goods and sweets;
		Drinks: see days 1 and 2
8	Emphasis on carbo- hydrates, easily	**Main energy sources:** whole grain products, vegetables, potatoes, rice, pasta, fruit;
9	digestible foods	**Supplemented with:** low fat milk and dairy products, little lean meat, poultry, fish, very little spreading and cooking fats, very few luxury good and sweets;
		Drinks: see days 1 and 2.

In practice this dietary and training principle in race week has worked very well and athletes have achieved top performances in races, although the side-effects mentioned cannot be completely excluded. It should also be noted that the considerably increased storage of glycogen in the muscles is accompanied by increased absorption of water (1 g glycogen binds 2.7 g water), so that a performance reducing weight increase is also possible (GEISS/HAMM 1992, 81)

Race Day

So as not to unnecessarily strain the bodily system with digestive work on race day the light, carbohydrate rich diet (65% of energy supply) of the super compensation phase is continued. A sufficient supply of fluids is of the greatest significance for performance capacity, therefore carbohydrate rich drinks are good for supplementing solid food intake. The supply of fat should be restricted to a maximum of 20% and protein should be at 10-15%.

What does this mean in practice?

In choosing food and beverages on race day it is important to consider what one personally finds easily digestible. The last major meal should be about three hours before the race. 45 to 60 minutes before the race a carbohydrate rich and low fat snack such as a muesli bar, a banana or a glass of fruit juice with soluble oat flakes is useful for stabilising the blood sugar level. 5 to 15 minutes before the race low calorie drinks are best for the covering of fluid needs.

Nourishment **during the race** is dependent on the duration of the race. Fluid intake comes first (still mineral water), as the body loses about 1.0 to 1.5 litres of water per hour. Energy drinks with up to 5% sugar solutions, such as diluted fruit juices, electrolyte drinks or cola, are also well-suited.

Secondly comes the consumption of fruit in very small amounts to ensure a constant supply of energy.

REGENERATION

Directly after the race the emphasis should be on fluid intake and refilling the glycogen stores in the liver and muscles through increased carbohydrate intake. In the following days one should also ensure sufficient protein consumption to compensate for possible wear and tear and a reduced amount of enzymes.

The more fat or alcohol consumed in this recovery phase the longer it takes to best refill the glycogen stores. The proportions of main nutrients in daily energy intake are the same as for the competition period (see Table 15).

Dietary Plan for a Female Duathlete in the Regeneration Phase

Example:
Female duathlete, age: 23 years, height: 173 cm, weight: 60 kg, training day during regeneration, 1 hour cycling (about 24 km/h), energy requirement: about 2,200 kcal (= 9.2 MJ) per day.

Proportion of main nutrients of food energy:

60-65% carbohydrates	=	330-358 g
20-25% fat	=	50-61 g
10-15% protein	=	77-88 g

Daily Recommendation for a Training Day during Regeneration

3 slices of wholemeal bread (120 g) and 2 slices mixed rye bread (80 g)	or	2 slices of wholemeal bread (80 g) and 20 g grain flakes (1 – 2 dsp)
150 g natural rice (cooked)	or	250 g potatoes (4 medium size)
200 g vegetables (steamed) and 100 g salad vegetables (raw)	or	150 g salad vegetable (raw) and 80 g legumes (cooked)
200 g fresh fruit and 200 g fruit juice	or	30 g dried fruits and 300 g fresh fruit
300 g milk (1.5% fat) 80 g curd cheese (20% fat) and 150 g yoghurt (1.5% fat)	or	200 g yoghurt (3.5% fat) and 1 slice of cheese (30% F.i.dr.m.) and 20 g cream cheese (1 dsp)
about 120 g lean meat, poultry or fish	or	about 60 g lean sliced sausage and 1 egg
15 g butter (3 – 4 tsp) and 10 g sunflower seed oil (1- 2 tsp)	or	25 g margarine (4 – 5 dsp)
20 g honey or jam (1 – 2 tsp)	or	10 g sugar (2 tsp) and 10 g honey or jam (1 – 2 tsp)

3 - 4 wholemeal biscuits (50 g)	*or*	1 bar of chocolate (20 g)
2 l mineral water and 1 l fruit tea	*or*	1 l fuit juice+mineral water (mixture juice to water 1:3) and 2 l mineral water

Abbreviations: dsp= desertspoon; tsp=teaspoon; F.i.dr.m.=fat in dry mass; l=litre

14.4.3 Transitional Period

This phase serves the build-up of energy suppliers and sufficient intake of essential nutrients to create performance prerequisites for the coming season. It is characterised by a balanced mixed diet slightly reduced in fat, and varies only slightly from the nutrient proportions of the preparatory period.

Here too the emphasis is on a balanced staple diet, i.e. the nutrition conscious duathlete should choose foodstuffs rich in nutrients to ensure his or her supply with vitamins and minerals. Furthermore, it has been proved that a balanced intake of carbohydrates, with plenty of roughage and a high fluid intake, have the effect of maintaining performance.

15 Setting up a Training Camp

15.1 Preparation

A training camp with a cycling emphasis requires special preparatory measures because during the winter months cycling training is often neglected, and the supportive and moving systems of the body are not used to a great degree of effort. In order to achieve measurable performance improvment from a training camp the following measures are imperative:

1. *Strength Training*

    Several weeks of strength training before a cycling training camp creates the muscular prerequisites for greater forward driving power, and increases the resilience of the supportive and movement system, which at the same time helps prevent injury (see chapter 11).

2. *Amount of Training*

    In the weeks before a cycling training camp a certain amount of training on the bike should be carried out to create the prerequisites for great strain on the system. Hobby athletes should cover at least 500 km, performance athletes at least 1,000 km and high performance athletes at least 1,500 km in the six weeks before the training camp begins. This can be done on a rolling machine, a bicycle ergometer, a mountain bike or a road bike.

3. *Injury Prevention*

    Strength training and the kilometres cycled before the training camp are the two most important pillars of injury prevention. As a rule, well-prepared athletes do not suffer the typical injuries of tendon inflammation (e.g. Achilles' tendon), inflammation of the bursa (e.g. in the knee joint), muscular tenseness and hardening (e.g. in the lower back muscles) or irritations to the tendon ends of the leg muscles.

15.2 Amount of Training and Cycling Preparations

The amount of training during a cycling course depends on the performance capacity and age of the athlete, the climatic conditions on location and the objectives. Assuming that a high degree of basic endurance capability is to be developed, young people and hobby athletes can cycle about 1,000 to 1,400 km, and performance athletes 1,400 to 1,800 km, during a 14 day training camp, as long as the above mentioned preparatory measures have been carried out.

Certainly greater amounts could be realised, but experience has shown that the main principles of exertion can then no longer be adhered to and the athlete can easily enter a state of overtraining. The desired effect of the training camp is then usually not achieved.

After the amount of training has been determined, the planning for each day is done. In doing so activities should be divided up according to the principle of cyclisation. For young people and hobby athletes a cycle of two days effort and one day recovery (2:1) has proven practical; performance athletes can train using a 3:1 or 4:1 cycle.

15.3 Practical Examples

We will now show the structuring of a cycling training camp with three women and eight men of the triathlon C squad. The example highlights the main training principles and emphasises the possibilities of professional training regulation.

The aim of the training work was to increase basic endurance capability in cycling. The coach laid down the amounts of daily effort, differentiated according to the individual performance level of the athletes.

15.3.1 Amount of Training

The total training time was divided between 84% cycling, 12% running and 4% swimming. The average daily training time was 4.6 h. This corresponded to a daily average of 100 cycling kilometres, 6 running kilometres and 0.5 swimming kilometres (Fig. 56).

Cycling Training Camp

Training Means and Training Amounts

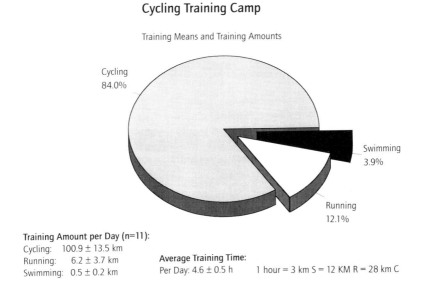

Cycling
84.0%

Swimming
3.9%

Running
12.1%

Training Amount per Day (n=11):
Cycling: 100.9 ± 13.5 km
Running: 6.2 ± 3.7 km   **Average Training Time:**
Swimming: 0.5 ± 0.2 km   Per Day: 4.6 ± 0.5 h   1 hour = 3 km S = 12 KM R = 28 km C

Fig. 56: *Training amounts at a cycling training camp with three women and eight men of the triathlon C squad*

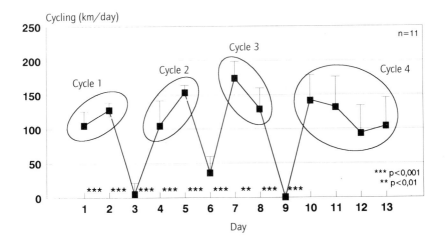

Fig. 57: *Structuring of training at a cycling training camp: cyclisation and training kilometres per day*

These average figures give an initial idea of training work. They do not, however, reflect the exertion structure of the course. For this, three BE 1 cycles with two days work and one day compensation/recovery and a final mixed training cycle with four days of work were chosen.

Fig. 57 shows the average amounts of cycling training in the individual cycles. According to this, the daily kilometres rise from about 100 km at the beginning to about 180 km on the 7th day (=greatest amount). On this day the training ride averaged 7.5 hours, some juniors covered 225 km.

15.3.2 Intensity of Training

Training intensity for the cycling training was determined using a cycling field test done on the first day. Each athlete was given their personal HR limit for the individual training regions. Because all athletes worked with HR measuring devices with memory (Polar Electro), checking intensity of effort was possible for both athletes and coach.

Fig. 58 shows an example of a BE 1 training session of about 7 h duration of the athlete S. Hachul. The heart rate limit values of the lower and upper BE 1 target region are 120 and 135 beats/min. A later analysis using the PC provides information on what percentage of the training session was within and outside the target region during training.

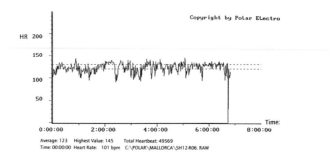

Fig. 58: Progression curve of heart rate of a duathlete during BE 1 cycling training over 180 km

Heart Rate Evaluation
of Cycling Training Session (C 01 – C 10)

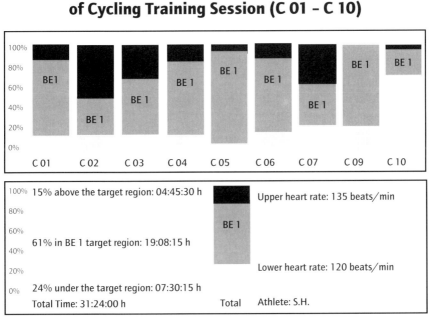

Fig. 59: Heart rate evaluation of the cycling training sessions of a duathlete during a 14 day training camp

Fig. 59 shows the calculation from nine cycling training sessions. It shows that of 31:24 training hours the athlete trained 61% in the target region of 120 to 135 beats/min, 24% under it and 15% above it. Training was therefore mainly in the lower intensity region.

In the following field stage test the athlete achieved the best performance within the squad team. In the 1994 German Triathlon Championships he had the fastest cycling time in the main class. The example once again underlines the great significance of the endurance foundation.

The athlete's organic strain and state of health were monitored with daily (morning) measurement of the pulse at rest, urea, creatin kinase and lactate.

The **pulse at rest** was determined palpatorily by the athletes themselves lying in bed in the morning. During the training days there were no changes in the pulse at rest.

Every morning the **urea values** were determined from the blood serum. The serum urea reading gives information on the activity of protein metabolism. High urea readings indicate that the carbohydrates and fats were not sufficient for gaining energy, and additional proteins had to be metabolised to maintain performance. Such great strains on the system must not take place several days in a row.

The high levels of training input led to a significant increase in urea after the first cycle. The following compensation day, with a swimming training session, lowered the raised urea level to the original values. One day of recovery thus sufficed to restore the greatly strained body.

The urea dynamic was repeated in a slightly less dramatic way in the second cycle of exertion. In the third cycle with the greatest amount of training, and also in the fourth, there were no more significant changes in the urea concentration. After about seven days the body had adjusted itself to the demands of training and reacted with less reduction and conversion of protein. The athletes had a higher resistance to strain.

Serum Urea

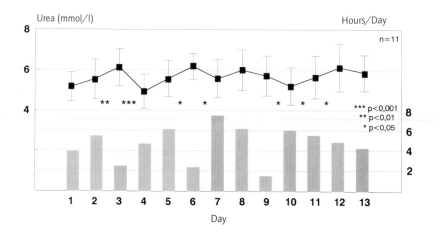

Fig. 60: *Average urea progression of 11 C squad triathletes during the cycling training camp*

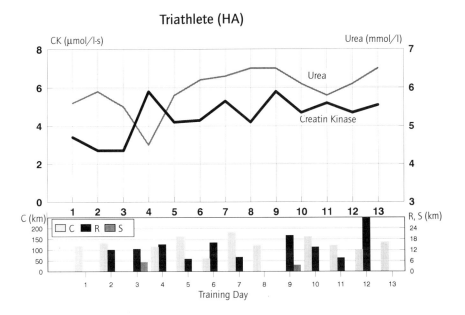

Fig. 61: Urea and creatin kinase progression of a 19 year old triathlete (explanation in text)

In order to get information on the athletes' muscular state the creatin kinase activity (CK) in the blood was ascertained. If the muscles are overtaxed, especially when there are muscle fibre injuries, the CK value rises.

During the training days the athletes had a wide range of differing reactions. An individual case analysis showed a rise in the CK values of those athletes who in addition to cycling training only sporadically went on long jogging runs. There were no changes among athletes who ran a few kilometres daily in addition to cycling training, not even when – in the case of Stefan Hachul – on the last day 28 km were run. It was a different picture for a training colleague, however, who had not run before but in the general euphoria also ran the 28 km. The next morning his CK value was 500% higher than the day before.

The results show in an impressive way that when changing the means of training certain principles must be strictly adhered to. Thus duathlon athletes should if possible also run daily during a cycling training camp. A run of 20-40 minutes straight after cycling training is recommended. The first kilometres should be in BE 2, the last kilometres in BE 1 or RECOM.

15.3.3 Case Studies

Training Camp for a performance oriented amateur athlete (< 5,000 cycling km per year)

Aim: Improve basic endurance ability in cycling

Training amount: about 1,200 - 1,400 cycling kilometres in two weeks

Cyclisation: 2:1 and 3:1, i.e. two (three) days of work and one day of recovery

1st Day:	Aim:	Active regeneration after the trip and acclimatisation
	AB:	Easy cycling trip (RECOM region) 2-3 hours on flat route
	AL:	Extensive jog (BE 1) 45-60 min
2nd Day:	Aim:	Determining of training intensities for basic endurance training
	AB:	Warm-up cycling 20 min., then cycling field test (e.g. 4 x 6,000 m) followed by 30 min cool down cycling
	AL:	Extensive cycle trip (BE 1) 2-3 hours coupled with an extensive jog (BE 1) over 20-30 min.
3rd Day:	Aim:	Recovery and regeneration Various regeneration measures (swimming 20-30 min., slow jog 30-45 min. or easy cycling trip 1-2 hours, mobility and coordination exercises, functional stretching and strengthening exercises, massage etc.)
4th Day:	Aim:	Development of basic endurance ability
	BB:	Easy jog (RECOM) 20-30 min., followed by running order exercises.

| | AB: | Extensive cycling trip (BE 1) 3-4 hours coupled with an intensive jog (BE 2) over 2-3 km. Finish with 15-20 min. easy cool down running. |

5th Day: Aim: Development of basic endurance ability

BB: Easy jog (RECOM) 20-30 min., followed by running gymnastics (Running order exercises).

AB: Long, extensive cycling trip (BE 1) 5-6 hours

6th Day: Aim: Recovery and regeneration (see 3rd day)

7th Day: Aim: Development of basic and strength endurance ability

AB: Extensive cycling trip (BE 1) 2-3 hours

AL: Extensive strength endurance cycling trip (SE 1) 1-2 hours, coupled with an intensive jog (BE 2) over 2-3 km, followed by 15-20 min easy cool down running

8th Day: Aim: Development of strength endurance ability

BB: Easy jog, 20-30 min followed by running gymnastics (running order exercises)

AB: Extensive cycling trip (BE 1) about one hour, then hill training (SE 2) e.g. 3-4 times 1-2 km with an active recovery sector of 2-3 km. After that continue the extensive cycling trip over 1-2 hours.

AL: Extensive jog (BE 1) 50-70 min

9th Day: Aim: Recovery and regeneration (see 3rd day)

10th Day: Aim: Development of basic endurance ability

BB: Easy jog, 20-30 min followed by running gymnastics (running order exercises)

| | AB: | Long, extensive cycling trip (BE 1) 4-5 hours, coupled with an intensive jog (BE 2) over 2-3 km. Afterwards 15-20 min easy cool down run |

11th day: Aim: Develop basic endurance ability

| | AB: | Long, extensive cycling trip (BE 1) over six hours (royal stage) |

12th Day: Aim: Recovery and regeneration (see 3rd day)

13th Day: Aim: Development of basic endurance ability

| | BB: | Easy jog, 20-30 min followed by running gymnastics (running order exercises) |

| | AB: | Extensive cycling trip (BE 1) about one hour, then speed training (BE 2) on relatively flat courses, e.g. 4-6 times 5 min with an active recovery break of 10 min. Afterwards continue the extensive cycling trip over 2-3 hours |

14th Day: Aim: Development of basic endurance ability

| | BB: | Easy jog, 20-30 min followed by running gymnastics (running order exercises) |

| | AB: | Long, extensive cycling trip (BE 1) using fartlek method, 5-7 hours on hilly courses |

Training camp for a performance athlete (> 5,000 cycling km per year)

Aim: Improve basic endurance ability in cycling

Training amount: 1,400 - 1,800 cycling kilometres in two weeks

Cyclisation: 2:1 and 3:1, i.e. two (three) days of work and one day of recovery

1st Day: Aim: Active regeneration after the trip and acclimatisation

	AB:	Easy cycling trip (RECOM region) 2-3 hours on flat route
	AL:	Extensive jog (BE 1) 50-70 min
2nd Day:	Aim:	Determining of training intensities for basic endurance training
	AB:	Warm-up cycling 30 min, then cycling field test (e.g. 4 x 6,000 m) followed by 60 min cool down cycling
	AL:	Extensive cycle trip (BE 1) 3-4 hours coupled with an extensive jog (BE 1) over 50-70 min
3rd Day:	Aim:	Development of basic endurance ability
	BB:	Easy jog (RECOM) 30-50 min, followed by running order exercises
	AB:	Extensive cycling trip (BE 1) 4-5 hours coupled with an intensive jog (BE 2) over 4-5 km. Finish with 15-20 min easy cool down running
4th Day:	Aim:	Recovery and regeneration
		Various regeneration measures (swimming 20-30 min, slow jog 40-60 min or easy cycling trip 1-2 hours, mobility and coordination exercises, functional stretching and strengthening exercises, massage etc.)
5th Day:	Aim:	Development of basic endurance ability
	AB:	Extensive cycling trip (BE 1) 5-6 hours coupled with an intensive jog (BE 2) over 4-5 km. Finish with 15-20 min easy cool down running
6th Day:	Aim:	Development of basic endurance ability
	BB:	Easy jog (RECOM) 20-30 min, followed by running gymnastics (running order exercises)

| | AB: | Long, extensive cycling trip (BE 1) 6-7 Std., coupled with an extensive jog (BE 1) over 50-60 min |

AB: Long, extensive cycling trip (BE 1) 6-7 Std., coupled with an extensive jog (BE 1) over 50-60 min

7th Day: Aim: Development of basic endurance ability

AB: Extensive cycling trip (BE 1) over eight hours (royal stage)

8th Day: Aim: Recovery and regeneration (see 4th day)

9th Day: Aim: Development of strength endurance ability

BB: Easy jog (RECOM) 20-30 min., followed by running gymnastics (running order exercises)

AB: Extensive strength endurance cycling trip (SE 1) 2-3 hours, coupled with an intensive jog (BE 2) over 5-6 km. Afterwards 15-20 min easy cool down run

10th Day: Aim: Development of strength endurance ability

BB: Easy jog, 20-30 min. followed by running gymnastics (running order exercises)

AB: Extensive cycling trip (BE 1) about one hour, then hill training (SE 2), e.g. 3-4 times 2-3 km with an active recovery sector of 2-3 km. After that continue the extensive cycling trip over 2-3 hours

AL: Extensive jog (BE 1) 50-70 min

11th day: Aim: Recovery and regeneration (see 4th a day)

12th Day: Aim: Develop basic endurance ability

BB: Easy jog, 40-50 min followed by running gymnastics (running order exercises)

	AB:	Extensive cycling trip (BE 1) 4-5 hours
	AL:	About 6-10 extensive 1,000 m runs (BE 2) with 600 m trotting break. Before and after the interval training at least 15 min easy running
13th Day:	Aim:	Development of strength and basic endurance ability
	BB:	Easy jog, 30-40 min followed by running gymnastics (running order exercises)
	AB:	Extensive strength endurance cycling trip (SE 1) about one hour, then speed training (BE 2), e.g. 4-5 times 10 min with an active recovery break of about 15 min. Afterwards at least an hour cool down cycling in extensive region (BE 1)
14th Day:	Aim:	Development of basic endurance ability
	AB:	Long, extensive cycling trip (BE 1) over seven hours using fartlek method

Functional stretching exercises have not been explicitly mentioned, but are a fixed component of daily training. In cycling training stretching exercises are particularly important after exertion (cf. chapter 4). A warm bath, massage or other physical meaures are recommended to relax the muscles.

Explanations:

BB: Before breakfast; AB: After breakfast; AL: After lunch

BE 1 Training: Pedalling rate of 90-120 r.p.m.

BE 2 Training: Pedalling rate of 80-90 r.p.m.

SE 1 Training: Pedalling rate of 50-70 r.p.m.

SE 2 Training: Pedalling rate of 40-60 r.p.m.

16. Muscle Soreness and Overtraining – A Result of Faulty Training?

16.1 Muscle Soreness

Symptoms

Practically everyone who has ever placed an unaccustomed amount of strain on their muscles during training or in a race knows this state: After one or two days the strained muscles feel hard and seem to react to every bit of pressure, every touch hurts. You don't dare think of movement, let alone renewed training, your weak muscles hurt too much for that. Who has not asked themselves in this situation: Where does this pain come from?

Theories

In the early days of sports medicine it was assumed that "muscle soreness" was a result of increased production of lactic acid (lactate) during exertion. Because this lactate was only removed from the muscles with some delay, so the theory that the lactic acid residue hindered the perfect functioning of the muscle and thus caused pain. Even today some still believe this theory although it is known that for example after a 400 m run the lactate concentration has reached normal levels after two hours at the latest, and you can still have muscle soreness the next day. According to the lactic acid theory the pain in the muscles should be greatest within a few minutes after crossing the finish line, for then the lactic acid level is highest. The so-called inflammation hypothesis too – overacidity in the muscles placed under strain leads to inflammation in the muscle, which then causes pain – similarly does not provide sufficient explanation for example for muscle soreness after a marathon run, in which only very low lactic acid concentrations arise. Therefore modern sports mediciners use the expression acute muscle soreness (AMS) to describe muscle pain which usually occurs during and immediately following exercise due to inadequate blood flow to active muscle and accumulation of metabolic waste products.

In 1956 ASMUSSEN discovered that not the lactate, but rather microscopically small tears in the aktin layers in the muscle fibres caused the pain of muscle soreness. This was later confirmed by electron microscopic examinations of muscle tissue. Muscle soreness which develops one or two days after exercise is therefore a mechanical damaging of individual parts of the muscle fibres (muscle fibrills).

Nowadays, the expression delayed on set muscle soreness (DOMS) describes the muscular discomfort caused by structural damage, to the muscle cells. DOMS usually occurs after strenuous, unaccustomed exercise and is greatest following eccentric training.

For this reason it should be clear to every athlete that remarks still heard today such as "After a real training session you have to suffer from DOMS" are **completely wrong**. On the contrary:

> ➡ **DOMS is in no way an indication of effective training, but rather an expression of faulty training.**

Treatment of DOMS:
1. rest or active recovery training.
2. Nonsteroidal duti-inflammatory drugs (NSAIDS) such as aspirin.

But how can DOMS be avoided?

1. By doing appropriate and correct warming-up and cooling down before and after every training session, but especially before intensive exertion (cf. chapter 4).

2. When new and unaccustomed loads (e.g. strength training, speed training) are initially applied at very low levels.

3. By avoiding unaccustomed, intensive and eccentric muscle work in a tired state.

4. By doing various forms of coupled training all year round (cf. chapter 8).

But faulty training can not only cause DOMS, it can cause a drop instead of an improvement in performance.

16.2 Overtraining

As already explained in chapter 5.3, overtraining is often connected with a training load that is too high. If these high demands are not complemented by sufficient breaks or recovery phases, the body is overtaxed. In this case the athlete trains with more or less emptied glycogen stores and can therefore no longer use the principle of super compensation to improve performance.

How does overtraining happen?

In general overtraining is preceded by symptoms of exhaustion over a longer period, which mostly result from a discrepancy between training and regeneration as well as between total strain and individual resilience. Of course not every feeling of tiredness is a sign of overtraining, but chronic tiredness should be cause for a longer training break. If hard training leads to local exhaustion of important energy depots, the so-called "first phase" or "peripheral tiredness", a two day break together with deliberate consumption of carbohydrates can help. If the state of physical unease and lack of training motivation do not improve, an additional "central tiredness" (second phase) and long-term overtraining may have arisen. In this case the athlete needs a longer period of regeneration as usually protein synthesis, i.e. the restoration processes, is also functioning more slowly than usual.

Diagnosis of Overtraining

All athletes can observe themselves and recognise first signs of avoidable overtraining. For example a reduction in performance capacity, an adding up of mistakes in coordination and technique as well as a reduction in strength on the one hand, a lack of desire to train, weak concentration, loss of appetite, sleeping problems, a rise in the pulse at rest and possibly weight loss on the other hand indicate overtraining. Unexpected illnesses can also arise because vulnerability to infection increases. Overtraining can, however, be avoided in the training process if athletes and coaches observe the main findings of training doctrines for endurance athletes.

> **Overtraining is an expression of faulty training and should**
> ➤ **always be avoided!**

The following is a summary of the major principles of endurance training, the "ten commandments for endurance athletes for the avoidance of faulty training", so to speak:

1. The structuring of exertion, accentuation of training objectives, the relationship between amount and intensity and the alternation of exertion and restoration must be individually adjusted in the training process and be subject to a constant dynamic.

2. In the structure of the year training should follow the dynamic increase in exertion from one period to the next until direct race preparation (DRP).

3. In order to process the greatest specific training loads, resilience should be increased in particular through all year training using general and semi-specific means.

4. The increase in basic and strength endurance should be continued on the basis of peaks of effort right into DRP.

5. An integration of specific characteristics of the main race in the year round training process avoids disruptive stimuli in DRP.

6. Cyclical structuring and a systematic ordering of training emphases create the basis for the structure of the year.

7. Within the training sections and stages the proportion of special training to general training should increase.

8. The phases of relief from strain or restoration after great training strain should not be too short as the relationship between strain and recovery has a substantial influence on adjustment, non-adjustment or overtraining.

9. Fewer, well-chosen races are recommended rather than too great a frequency of races.

10. Diet should be adjusted to the demands specific to the sport in the individual training periods.

17 Bibliography

Bauersfeld, K.-H., Schröter, G.: Grundlagen der Leichtathletik. Sportverlag, Berlin 1979.

Betz, M.: Triathlon im Kindesalter. Czwalina, Hamburg 1993.

Bremer, D., Engelhardt, M., Hottenrott, K., Neumann, G., Pfützner, A.: Triathlon: Orthopädische und internistische Aspekte. Czwalina Verlag, Ahrensburg bei Hamburg 1993.

DGE (Deutsche Gesellschaft für Ernährung) (Hrsg.): Empfehlungen für die Nährstoffzufuhr, Umschau Verlag, Frankfurt a.M. 1992.

Engelhardt, M., Kremer, A.: Triathlon perfekt. BLV Verlagsgesellschaft, München 1987.

Engelhardt, M. (Hrsg.): Erfolgreiches Triathlon Training. BLV Verlagsgesellschaft, München 1994.

Engelhardt, M., Neumann, G.: Sportmedizin für alle Ausdauersportarten. BLV Verlagsgesellschaft, München 1994.

Engelhardt, M.: Duathlon. Rowohlt-Verlag, Reinbek b. Hamburg 1993.

Freiwald, J.: Aufwärmen im Sport. Rowohlt Verlag, Reinbek bei Hamburg 1991.

Fuchs, V., Reiß, M.: Höhentraining. Philippka Verlag, Münster 1990.

Farrow, J.A.: The Adolescent Male with an Eating Disorder. In: Pediatric annals 21 (1992), 769-774.

Frey, G., Hildenbrandt, E.: Einführung in die Trainingslehre. Teil 1: Grundlagen. Hofmann-Verlag, Schorndorf 1994.

Geiß K.R., Hamm, M.: Handbuch Sportler Ernährung. Rowohlt Verlag, Reinbek b. Hamburg 1992.

Grosser, M.: Training der konditionellen Fähigkeiten. Hofmann-Verlag, Schorndorf 1989.

Hamm M., Weber, M.: Sporternährung praxisnah. Hädecke Verlag, Weil der Stadt 1988.

Hottenrott, K.: Trainingssteuerung im Ausdauersport. Czwalina Verlag, Ahrensburg bei Hamburg 1993.

Hottenrott, K.: Ausdauertraining. Verlag Wehdemeier & Pusch, 1994.

Hottenrott, K., Zülch, M.: Ausdauerprogramme. Erfolgstraining für alle Sportarten. Rowohlt Verlag, Reinbeck, b. Hamburg 1995.

Jakowlew, N. N.: Ermüdung im Sport: Grundlagen und Bedeutung. Leistungssport 8 (1978) 6, 513-516.

Klimt, F.: Sportmedizin im Kindes- und Jugendalter. Thieme, Stuttgart-New York 1992.

Knebel, K.-P.: Funktionsgymnastik. Rowohlt Verlag, Reinbek b. Hamburg 1994.

Kunz, H.-R., Schneider, W., Spring, H., Tritschler, T, Inauen, E. U.: Krafttraining. Georg Thieme Verlag, Stuttgart - New York 1990.

Lehmann, M.: Übertraining im Ausdauersport. In: Bremer, D., Engelhardt, M., Hottenrott, K., Neumann, G., Pfützner, A.: Triathlon: Orthopädische und internistische Aspekte. Czwalina Verlag, Ahrensburg bei Hamburg 1993, 85-90.

Lindner, W.: Erfolgreiches Radsporttraining. Vom Amateur zum Profi. BLV Verlagsgesellschaft, München 1993.

Martin, D.: Training im Kindes- und Jugendalter. Hofmann, Schorndorf 1988.

Martin, D. (Red.), Carl, K., Lehnertz, K.: Handbuch Trainingslehre. Verlag Hofmann, Schorndorf 1991.

McArdle W.D., Katch, F. I., Katch, V. L.: Exercise Physiology: Energy Nutrition and Human Performance. Lea & Febiger, Philadelphia 1985.

Medau, I I. J., Nowacki, P. E.: Frau und Sport. Perimed Fachbuch-Verlagsgesellschaft mbH, Erlangen 1983.

Meermann, R., Vandereycken, W.: Therapie der Magersucht und Bulimia nervosa. Walter de Gruyter, Berlin - New York 1987.

Müller, K.W., Ernst, J., Strasser, H.: Statische und dynamische Komponenten des EMG bei repetitiven Bewegungsabläufen. In: Daugs, R., Leist, K.-H., Ulmer, H.-V.: Motorikforschung aktuell. Aktuelle Beiträge zur Motorikforschung. DVS, Clausthal-Zellerfeld 1989, 21-26.

Neumann, G.: Organismische Anpassungsgrenze erreicht? TW Sport + Medizin 3 (1991) 46-52.

Neumann, G.: Sportmedizinische Standpunkte zur Wettkampfvorbereitung in Ausdauersportarten. Leistungssport 24 (1994) 1, 49-52.

Neumann, G., Pfützner, A., Hottenrott, K.: Alles unter Kontrolle. Meyer & Meyer Verlag, Aachen 1993.

Neumann, G., Berbalk, A.: Umstellung und Anpassung des Organismus - grundlegende Voraussetzungen der sportlichen Leistungsfähigkeit. In: Bernett, P., Jeschke, D. (Hrsg.): Sport und Medizin - Pro und Contra. Zuckschwerdt, München 1991, 415-419.

Pfützner, A.: Kraftausdauertraining im Triathlon. In: Bremer D., Engelhardt, M., Hottenrott, K., Neumann, G., Pfützner, A.: Triathlon: Orthopädische und internistische Aspekte. Czwalina Verlag, Hamburg 1993, 115-125.

Pfützner, A., Große, S., Baldauf, K., Gohlitz, D., Witt, M.: Koppeltraining - Hauptbestandteil einer triathlonspezifischen Fähigkeitsentwicklung. In: Engelhardt M., Franz, B., Neumann, G., Pfützner, A.: Triathlon: Medizinische und methodische Probleme des Trainings. Czwalina Verlag, Hamburg 1994, 101-122.

Pickenhain, L., Neumann, G., Scharschmidt, F.: Sportmedizin. Verlag Hans Huber, Bern - Göttingen - Seattle - Toronto 1993.

Reiß, M., Pfeiffer, U. (Hrsg.): Leistungsreserven im Ausdauertraining. Sportverlag, Berlin 1991.

Roß, A.: Magersucht - Wenn Läuferinnen nicht mehr essen. Runners World 6 (1994), 62-65.

Schenk, S. (Hrsg.): Frauen, Bewegung, Sport. VSA-Verlag, Hamburg 1986.

Schnabel, G., Harre, D., Borde, A. (Hrsg.): Trainingswissenschaft. Sportverlag Berlin 1994.

Sommer, H. M., Rohrscheidt, Ch. v., Arza, D.: Leistungssteigerung und Prophylaxe von Überlastung und Verletzung des Haltungs- und Bewegungsapparates im Sport durch "Alternative" Gymnastik. Leichtathletik 51/52 (1987) 1763-1766.

Spring, H., Illi, U., Kunz, H.-R., Röthlin, K., Schneider, W., Tritschler, T.: Dehn- und Kräftigungsgymnastik. Thieme Verlag, Stuttgart New York 1986.

Steffny, M.: Marathon-Training. Verlag Hermann Schmidt, Mainz 1991.

Tiedemann, P.: Der Mythos vom schwachen Geschlecht. In: Schenk, S. (Hrsg.): Frauen, Bewegung, Sport. VSA-Verlag, Hamburg 1986, 77-84.

Weineck, J.: Optimales Training. PERIMED-spitta, Med. Verlagsgesellschaft Balingen 1994.

Speed Table – Cycling

V (km/h)	V (min/km)	V (m/s)	Time 2 km [mm:ss]	Time 3 km	Time 5 km	Time 10 km	Time 40 km [hh:mm]	Time 90 km	Time 180 km
25	2: 24	6,9	4: 48	7: 12	12: 00	24: 00	1: 36	3: 36	7: 12
26	2: 18	7,2	4: 37	6: 55	11: 32	23: 05	1: 32	3: 28	6: 55
27	2: 13	7,5	4: 27	6: 40	11: 07	22: 13	1: 29	3: 20	6: 40
28	2: 09	7,8	4: 17	6: 26	10: 43	21: 26	1: 26	3: 13	6: 26
29	2: 04	8,1	4: 08	6: 12	10: 21	20: 41	1: 23	3: 06	6: 12
30	2: 00	8,3	4: 00	6: 00	10: 00	20: 00	1: 20	3: 00	6: 00
31	1: 56	8,6	3: 52	5: 48	9: 41	19: 21	1: 17	2: 54	5: 48
32	1: 53	8,9	3: 45	5: 38	9: 23	18: 45	1: 15	2: 49	5: 38
33	1: 49	9,2	3: 38	5: 27	9: 05	18: 11	1: 13	2: 44	5: 27
34	1: 46	9,4	3: 32	5: 18	8: 49	17: 39	1: 11	2: 39	5: 18
35	1: 43	9,7	3: 26	5: 09	8: 34	17: 09	1: 09	2: 34	5: 09
36	1: 40	10,0	3: 20	5: 00	8: 20	16: 40	1: 07	2: 30	5: 00
37	1: 37	10,3	3: 15	4: 52	8: 06	16: 13	1: 05	2: 26	4: 52
38	1: 35	10,6	3: 09	4: 44	7: 54	15: 47	1: 03	2: 22	4: 44
39	1: 32	10,8	3: 05	4: 37	7: 42	15: 23	1: 02	2: 18	4: 37
40	1: 30	11,1	3: 00	4: 30	7: 30	15: 00	1: 00	2: 15	4: 30
41	1: 28	11,4	2: 56	4: 23	7: 19	14: 38	0: 59	2: 12	4: 23
42	1: 26	11,7	2: 51	4: 17	7: 09	14: 17	0: 57	2: 09	4: 17
43	1: 24	11,9	2: 47	4: 11	6: 59	13: 57	0: 56	2: 06	4: 11
44	1: 22	12,2	2: 44	4: 05	6: 49	13: 38	0: 55	2: 03	4: 05
45	1: 20	12,5	2: 40	4: 00	6: 40	13: 20	0: 53	2: 00	4: 00
46	1: 18	12,8	2: 37	3: 55	6: 31	13: 03	0: 52	1: 57	3: 55
47	1: 17	13,1	2: 33	3: 50	6: 23	12: 46	0: 51	1: 55	3: 50
48	1: 15	13,3	2: 30	3: 45	6: 15	12: 30	0: 50	1: 53	3: 45
49	1: 13	13,6	2: 27	3: 40	6: 07	12: 15	0: 49	1: 50	3: 40
50	1: 12	13,9	2: 24	3: 36	6: 00	12: 00	0: 48	1: 48	3: 36

Speed Table – Running

V (min/km)	V (km/h)	V (m/s)	Time 200 m [mm:ss]	Time 300 m	Time 400 m	Time 1,500 m	Time 3,000 m	Time 5,000 m	Time 10,000m	Time 42. 195 km [hh:mm]
06:00	10,0	2,8	1:12	1:48	2:24	9:00	18:00	30:00	60:00	4:13
05:55	10,1	2,8	1:11	1:47	2:23	8:55	17:49	29:42	59:24	4:11
05:50	10,3	2,9	1:10	1:45	2:20	8:44	17:29	29:08	58:15	4:06
05:45	10,4	2,9	1:09	1:44	2:18	8:39	17:18	28:51	57:42	4:03
05:40	10,6	2,9	1:08	1:42	2:16	8:29	16:59	28:18	56:36	3:59
05:35	10,7	3,0	1:07	1:41	2:15	8:25	16:49	28:02	56:04	3:57
05:30	10,9	3,0	1:06	1:39	2:12	8:15	16:31	27:31	55:03	3:52
05:25	11,1	3,1	1:05	1:37	2:10	8:06	16:13	27:02	54:03	3:48
05:20	11,3	3,1	1:04	1:36	2:07	7:58	15:56	26:33	53:06	3:44
05:15	11,4	3,2	1:03	1:35	2:06	7:54	15:47	26:19	52:38	3:42
05:10	11,6	3,2	1:02	1:33	2:04	7:46	15:31	25:52	51:43	3:38
05:05	11,8	3,3	1:01	1:32	2:02	7:38	15:15	25:25	50:51	3:35
05:00	12,0	3,3	1:00	1:30	2:00	7:30	15:00	25:00	50:00	3:31
04:55	12,2	3,4	0:59	1:29	1:58	7:23	14:45	24:35	49:11	3:28
04:50	12,4	3,4	0:58	1:27	1:56	7:15	14:31	24:12	48:23	3:24
04:45	12,6	3,5	0:57	1:26	1:54	7:09	14:17	23:49	47:37	3:21
04:40	12,9	3,6	0:56	1:24	1:52	6:59	13:57	23:15	46:31	3:16
04:35	13,1	3,6	0:55	1:22	1:50	6:52	13:44	22:54	45:48	3:13
04:30	13,3	3,7	0:54	1:21	1:48	6:46	13:32	22:33	45:07	3:10
04:25	13,6	3,8	0:53	1:19	1:46	6:37	13:14	22:04	44:07	3:06
04:20	13,8	3,8	0:52	1:18	1:44	6:31	13:03	21:44	43:29	3:03
04:15	14,1	3,9	0:51	1:17	1:42	6:23	12:46	21:17	42:33	2:60
04:10	14,4	4,0	0:50	1:15	1:40	6:15	12:30	20:50	41:40	2:56
04:05	14,7	4,1	0:49	1:13	1:38	6:07	12:15	20:24	40:49	2:52
04:00	15,0	4,2	0:48	1:12	1:36	6:00	12:00	20:00	40:00	2:49
03:55	15,3	4,3	0:47	1:11	1:34	5:53	11:46	19:36	39:13	2:45
03:50	15,7	4,4	0:46	1:09	1:32	5:44	11:28	19:06	38:13	2:41
03:45	16,0	4,4	0:45	1:08	1:30	5:38	11:15	18:45	37:30	2:38
03:40	16,4	4,6	0:44	1:06	1:28	5:29	10:59	18:18	36:35	2:34
03:35	16,7	4,6	0:43	1:05	1:26	5:23	10:47	17:58	35:56	2:32
03:30	17,1	4,8	0:42	1:03	1:24	5:16	10:32	17:33	35:05	2:28
03:25	17,6	4,9	0:41	1:01	1:22	5:07	10:14	17:03	34:05	2:24
03:20	18,0	5,0	0:40	1:00	1:20	5:00	10:00	16:40	33:20	2:21
03:15	18,5	5,1	0:39	0:58	1:18	4:52	9:44	16:13	32:26	2:17
03:10	18,9	5,3	0:38	0:57	1:16	4:46	9:31	15:52	31:45	2:14
03:05	19,5	5,4	0:37	0:55	1:14	4:37	9:14	15:23	30:46	2:10
03:00	20,0	5,6	0:36	0:54	1:12	4:30	9:00	15:00	30:00	2:07

Heart rate table (% values of maximum heart rate)

HR max	95	93	91	90	88	85	78	75	73	70	68	65	63	60
210	200	195	191	189	185	179	164	158	153	147	143	137	132	126
208	198	193	189	187	183	177	162	156	152	146	141	135	131	125
206	196	192	187	185	181	175	161	155	150	144	140	134	130	124
204	194	190	186	184	180	173	159	153	149	143	139	133	129	122
202	192	188	184	182	178	172	158	152	147	141	137	131	127	121
200	190	186	182	180	176	170	156	150	146	140	136	130	126	120
198	188	184	180	178	174	168	154	149	145	139	135	129	125	119
196	186	182	178	176	172	167	153	147	143	137	133	127	123	118
194	184	180	177	175	171	165	151	146	142	136	132	126	122	116
192	182	179	175	173	169	163	150	144	140	134	131	125	121	115
190	181	177	173	171	167	162	148	143	139	133	129	124	120	114
188	179	175	171	169	165	160	147	141	137	132	128	122	118	113
186	177	173	169	167	164	158	145	140	136	130	126	121	117	112
184	175	171	167	166	162	156	144	138	134	129	125	120	116	110
182	173	169	166	164	160	155	142	137	133	127	124	118	115	109
180	171	167	164	162	158	153	140	135	131	126	122	117	113	108
178	169	166	162	160	157	151	139	134	130	125	121	116	112	107
176	167	164	160	158	155	150	137	132	128	123	120	114	111	106
174	165	162	158	157	153	148	136	131	127	122	118	113	110	104
172	163	160	157	155	151	146	134	129	126	120	117	112	108	103
170	162	158	155	153	150	145	133	128	124	119	116	111	107	102
168	160	156	153	151	148	143	131	126	123	118	114	109	106	101
166	158	154	151	149	146	141	129	125	121	116	113	108	105	100
164	156	153	149	148	144	139	128	123	120	115	112	107	103	98
162	154	151	147	146	143	138	126	122	118	113	110	105	102	97
160	152	149	146	144	141	136	125	120	117	112	109	104	101	96
158	150	147	144	142	139	134	123	119	115	111	107	103	100	95
156	148	145	142	140	137	133	122	117	114	109	106	101	98	94
154	146	143	140	139	136	131	120	116	112	108	105	100	97	92
152	144	141	138	137	134	129	119	114	111	106	103	99	96	91
150	143	140	137	135	132	128	117	113	110	105	102	98	95	90